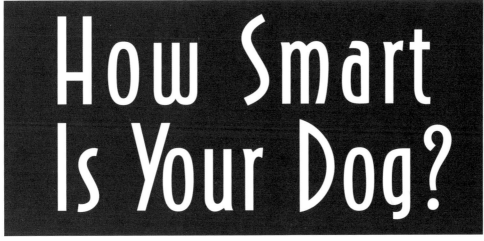

# How Smart Is Your Dog?

## 30 Fun Science Activities with Your Pet

D. Caroline Coile, Ph.D.

illustrations by Catherine Leary

Sterling Publishing Co., Inc.
New York

Book design by *Spinning Egg Design Group, Inc.*
Edited by Isabel Stein.

**Library of Congress Cataloging-in-Publication Data Available**

10 9 8 7 6 5 4 3 2 1

Published by Sterling Publishing Co., Inc.
387 Park Avenue South, New York, N.Y. 10016
© 2003 by D. Caroline Coile
Distributed in Canada by Sterling Publishing
c/o Canadian Manda Group, One Atlantic Avenue, Suite 105
Toronto, Ontario, Canada M6K 3E7
Distributed in Great Britain and Europe by Chris Lloyd at Orca Book
Services, Stanley House, Fleets Lane, Poole BH15 3AJ, England
Distributed in Australia by Capricorn Link (Australia) Pty. Ltd.
P.O. Box 704, Windsor, NSW 2756  Australia

*Printed in China*
*All rights reserved*

Sterling  ISBN 0-8069-7677-2

# CONTENTS

# CONTENTS

# Introduction: Be Your Dog's Best Friend

**W**elcome to the world of cynology, the study of dogs! Do you love dogs? Even if you don't have a dog, you can still have fun learning about them. If you have a dog, ask yourself how well you really know your dog. Did you know that you and your dog see, smell and hear the world around you very differently? Your dog can probably understand a little English; how well can you understand doglish? Can you tell when your dog is sick? Can you tell when she is happy?

This book will help you get to know how her body works, how she perceives the world, what she's thinking, and how she feels. It will help you understand your dog not just by reading about dogs, but by exploring your dog through various fun and educational activities. It will help you be as good a friend to her as she is to you.

Do you dream of becoming a veterinarian? This book will give you a head start. It will lead you through demonstrations and experiments that will show you how your dog works and what she can do.

You may be interested in one of the other careers with dogs given in the section at the end of the book. You may simply want to be the best friend to your dog you can be. But whatever you choose, the first step is getting to know all about dogs.

# Canine Mysteries

Just in case you think there's nothing left to discover about dogs, we're happy to tell you there's plenty. It's just as important for you to ask questions as it is to answer them. For many years people asked if dogs were color-blind; now we know they're not — although they do see colors differently from the way we see them.

Here are some unsolved mysteries:

- Why do dogs turn in a circle before they lie down?
- Why do dogs roll in disgusting things?
- Can dogs predict earthquakes? If so, how?
- Can dogs smell fear?
- Why do some dogs bite?
- How do dogs follow a trail?
- Can dogs really find their way home if they're lost hundreds of miles away?
- Do dogs have ESP?

As you read through this book, and as you spend time with your dog, keep a notepad handy to jot down questions that occur to you. Maybe one day you will be the one to answer them!

Many scientists and veterinarians are working to improve the health of our canine friends. Understanding how the dog's body works is the first step to keeping her healthy. One day you may be the person to make a new discovery that will save dogs' lives.

## About the Book

This book is designed so you can skip around and read the parts that interest you. The only section you should read first is Before You Start (but that's kind of obvious). You may also want to learn the external anatomy of the dog before getting started (page 18).

The book is divided into four sections. The first, Your Dog's Body, describes the physical characteristics of dogs. The second part, Your Dog's World, describes how your dog sees, hears, smells, tastes, and touches the world around her. The third part, Inside Your Dog's Mind, describes the dog's brain, intelligence, memory, and learning, as well as some of the jobs of dogs. The fourth part, Your Dog's Health and Functioning, describes some ways you can keep your dog as healthy as possible and gives some fun activities to do with your dog.

## The Activities

Doing an activity or experiment with your dog isn't like doing one with mold or chemicals. Like people, dogs are individuals; no two are alike. What works well for one dog may not go as smoothly for another. Dogs are living, feeling, thinking beings who, like you, have emotions and moods and good days and bad days.

# NEAT TREATS

Many of the projects in this book involve food treats. A few of them require lots and lots of treats — maybe 100 treats in a day for some of the training experiments! In that case you need to choose a treat that is very small so your dog won't take all day eating it and won't get fat from eating so many. A treat should be no larger than the end of your thumb.

One good treat is dry kitten or cat food; it's small and tasty and easy to carry. The semi-moist dog food that comes in plastic pouches also makes good treats, but you may have to cut it into smaller pieces. If your dog is picky you can use cheese, cooked liver, or the type of food that is sold in rolls at pet supermarkets. Dogs love those! But no chocolate. Chocolate contains an ingredient that is fine for people but can be poisonous to dogs.

If your dog is old or on a special diet, check with your veterinarian first to make sure the treat is not unhealthy for him. You can clip a plastic bag to your belt to hold treats so you don't mess up your pockets. If you carry food in your pocket, clean out your pocket and don't leave your clothes where your dog can find them; dogs have been known to chew through pants to get to the crumbs in their pockets!

I've tried each of these experiments with my own dogs. On some days they had me convinced their brains must have fallen out on the ground. It's easy to lose your patience when that happens, but this is one time when being a quitter is best. Just come back later when you're both in a better mood. Sometimes just changing when you train can help. If you train your dog before he eats, he'll be hungry and will be more likely to work for treats. Full, tired, hot, ill, or distracted dogs are hard to train. Wait until they are hungry, alert, comfortable, well and focused on you.

Many of these experiments would make excellent science fair projects. Before choosing one for a science fair, however, make sure your science fair's rules allow projects with dogs. Consult your teacher and be sure you get approval before you start. Some science fairs don't allow any experiments with animals because of concern that the animals will be harmed.

None of the experiments in this book is harmful to your dog. No punishment, deprivation, or force should be used. Remember, these experiments are supposed to be fun for both you and your dog!

Please review the safety instructions on the following pages before you start. Then call your dog to you, settle down together, and start getting to know one another!

# Before You Start: Safety Tips for You and Your Parents

The activities described in this book are designed to be safe with healthy, well-adjusted dogs. However, no dog is 100% predictable. All dogs are capable of biting. Nobody knows your dog better than you do. Please remember:

- Use only a dog you know and trust for these activities.
- Dogs that have behaved aggressively in the past should not be used in these activities.
- An adult should be present to help or supervise during all activities, especially ones that require the person doing the experiment to be near the dog's face.
- Only one dog at a time should be present during any activity.
- If the dog becomes frightened or irritated, stop the activity.
- If the dog starts barking at or acting aggressively toward a visitor or another animal, stop the activity.
- No dog should ever be left alone with a child who is not at least twice as large as the dog.
- Visiting children should not play roughly around household dogs, who may think the children are fighting.
- Your dog's safety is equally important. If your dog is old, has a painful condition, or is ill, pregnant, or nursing puppies, you should consult your veterinarian before including her in your experiments. These dogs may not be able to participate in experiments requiring changes in exercise or diet. Pregnant and nursing dogs should only be included in simple studies where you observe their behavior.

# How to Avoid Dog Bites

Everyone should be familiar with the following dog safety rules:

- Never approach a loose dog.
- Never pet a dog without the owner's permission.
- Never approach a dog with puppies.
- Never tease a dog that is chained up or behind a fence.
- Never put your hand through a fence to pet a strange dog.

**How to approach and pet a strange dog.**

- Never enter a yard with a dog in it without permission.
- Never put your hand between two strange dogs, or any dogs that look like they may fight.
- Never get in the middle of a bunch of dogs.
- Never try to break up a dogfight.
- Never try to touch a strange dog that has been injured or who is in pain.
- Never approach a dog that is eating or that is chewing a bone.
- Never approach a scared dog.
- Never bother or surprise a sleeping dog.
- Never try to take a toy away from a strange dog, even if it's your toy.

- Never place your face near the face of a strange dog.
- Never run toward, away from, or anywhere around a strange dog.
- Never make loud shrieks around a strange dog.
- Never stare a strange dog in the eye.
- Never assume that a wagging tail means a friendly dog.

## What to Do If a Dog Menaces You

- If a dog acts menacing to you, stand still. Fold your arms across your chest and look away from the dog. Speak in a low-pitched calm voice. Back away slowly. Do not run or scream.

- If a dog chases you on your bicycle, stop the bike and get off. Keep the bike between you and the dog. Walk away slowly.

- If a dog starts to come after you, give him anything you have — your lunch, your toys, your books, or your backpack — to distract him. Throw the item to the side so he doesn't think you're trying to hit him with it.

- If a dog starts to chase you and you have a way to make a loud noise such as with a horn or whistle, make that noise. Do not scream.

- If a dog attacks you, cover your face and neck; try to remain standing and get to a safe place, such as inside a car, on the other side of a fence, or even on a car or up a tree.

- If a dog knocks you down, curl up in a ball and cover your face and neck with your hands. Do not scream.

## How to Say It

Standing safety position and safety position on ground.

Some of the words in this book are long and pretty hard to say, so there are HOW TO SAY IT lists that spell out how to pronounce difficult words. Instead of using all the weird symbols they use in the dictionary to pronounce words, I just spelled them as they sound and put the syllables that are to be accented in all capital letters. The words in the HOW TO SAY IT sections are marked with an asterisk* (little star) the first time they appear in the text. Here's one word for this section: **Cynology: sie-NAHL-oh-jee.**

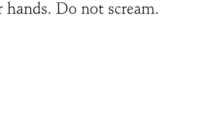

**11**

# Signs of an Aggressive Dog

- Posture is erect.
- Head is held up.
- Eyes stare right at you.
- Lips are curled back and up.
- Growls may be heard.
- Hair on shoulders and back stands up.
- Tail is held up.
- Movement is stiff-legged.

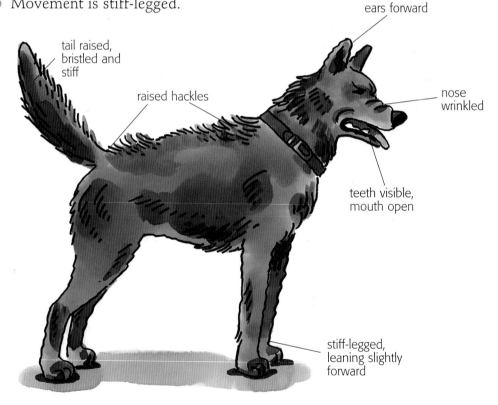

ears forward

tail raised,
bristled and
stiff

raised hackles

nose
wrinkled

teeth visible,
mouth open

stiff-legged,
leaning slightly
forward

Signs of an aggressive dog.

FAMILY TREE

Grandma
Sara
Wolf

Grampa
Willy
Wolf

# Your Dog's Body

**B**ig dogs, little dogs, fluffy dogs, and hairless dogs — dogs come in more sizes and shapes than any other mammal. But they all evolved from some type of wolf. Trace the dog's prehistory, take a look at some of his relatives, and then meet some of today's dogs. Get to know your dog from the tip of his cold nose to the end of his wagging tail, inside and out, and do some neat experiments along the way.

Look out! There may be a wolf in your house.... All dogs alive today are descended from wolves. Scientists classify all living things into different family groupings, based on how they are related to each other. To do this, they use evidence from fossils, physical traits, behavior, and DNA (genetic material in body cells transmitted from generation to generation). This evidence places wolves and dogs in the mammal group, which includes all animals that have hair and nurse their young. Wolves, dogs, cats, bears, and some other groups of mammals are part of the scientific order of carnivores (Carnivora). Carnivores are mammals who have special features that help them to hunt for and eat other animals. We'll learn more about carnivores later.

Dogs, foxes, jackals, and wolves belong to the family of carnivores called Canidae — the dog family. (Canis is Latin for "dog.") In English they're called canids.* There are 35 species in the dog family.

The dog's scientific classification shows that it is closely related to the gray wolf *(Canis lupus)*.

Class: Mammalia
Order: Carnivora
Family: Canidae
Genus: Canis
Species: *Canis lupus familiaris** or *Canis familiaris*

## THE DOG'S EARLY ANCESTORS

Dogs, coyotes, wolves, and foxes belong to the Canidae* (dog) family, so they're all called canids* in English. The first canid-like creature, Hesperocyon* ("western dog"), appeared about 55 to 35 million years ago in North America. It had a long body and short legs. The first coyote-like creature, Eucyon* ("true dog"), appeared around 10 million years ago. Eucyon's descendents gave rise to the modern wolves about one million years ago.

## How to SAY IT

**canid:** KAY-ned

**Canidae:** CAN-ih-die

**Canis lupus familiaris:** KANE-is LOO-pus fah-MIL-ee-AIR-is

**Hesperocyon:** hess-PAIR-o-SY-on

**Eucyon:** YOU-sy-on

It isn't known yet whether dogs are a subspecies of wolves or a separate species, *Canis familiaris*. People are still trying to discover when the first dogs were domesticated (raised to live with and help humans). There are fossils showing dog and human skeletons together as far back as 14,000

**ACTIVITY**

**YOU WILL NEED:**
- shallow container (such as a pie tin or ice cream carton)
- two mixing containers such as empty large juice cartons or large yogurt containers
- old paintbrush
- enough damp sand (or clay) to fill the container about 2 inches deep
- water
- plaster of Paris mix, about a cup (250 mL)
- cooking oil or Vaseline

# Make a Good Impression

Much of what we know about the dog's ancestors comes from fossil evidence, either fossilized bones or footprints. By looking at the animals' bones, teeth, and footprints, we can learn many things about how they moved and what they ate. Some footprints were made in mud that later turned to rock. You can make fossil footprints from your dog's feet.

1. Pack the damp sand in the bottom of the container.

2. Press the dog's foot deep into the sand.

3. Take his foot out; make sure he left a good footprint.

4. Mix water with plaster according to the instructions on the box.

5. Pour a layer of plaster over the entire surface of the sand. (Note: Do not pour the leftover plaster down the sink. It will clog the pipes. Let it dry in the container and throw it out.)

6. Let the plaster you poured dry for about an hour.

7. Remove the plaster shape and dust off loose sand and plaster pieces. You will have a mold fossil, which is a negative impression of the footprint.

8. To make a cast fossil, a fossil that looks like the original footprint, coat the negative mold fossil (plaster paw) with cooking oil or Vaseline and place it back in the shallow container upside down, so the paw shape sticks up from the base. (The oil between the old and new plaster acts as a separator. Brush it on with an old paintbrush.)

9. Mix some more plaster and pour it over the hard plaster paw so it covers the paw shape.

10. Let it dry. Carefully separate the two pieces and remove any oil or Vaseline. Your new fossil is like the original footprint.

years ago, while people were still hunters and gatherers. DNA evidence suggests dogs evolved from wolves as long as 100,000 years ago. This means that dogs were the first animals to be domesticated.

Dogs may have been bred and trained to act as hunters, guards, scavengers, as sources of food or warmth, and as companions. People may have first taken orphan wolf cubs to raise as pets. Then again, wolves may have domesticated themselves. It's possible that when early humans started to live in settlements, some brave wolves started to hang around and eat people's trash. Wolves that weren't too afraid of being near people were able to eat their fill from the trash pile, breed with each other, and produce more tame wolves. In time, a new type of tame wolf gradually may have evolved.

## Wild Dogs

Wolves are not the only wild canids. Wild canids are native to every continent except Antarctica and Australia — and Australia is home to the dingo, a wild canid developed from dogs. There are about 35 species of wild canids. They include wolves, jackals, and foxes. Here are some:

- The gray wolf *(Canis lupus)* is the largest and most social wild canid. Its territory has been greatly reduced; now the gray wolf is found mostly in parts of Canada and the northern United States, and Russia.

- The coyote *(Canis latrans)* is actually expanding its territory. It can now be found in rural and even suburban areas throughout most of the United States and Mexico.

- The dingo *(Canis lupus dingo)* was originally a domestic dog. It reverted to the wild thousands of years ago. It is considered a pest in much of Australia.

- The golden jackal *(Canis aureus)* is found throughout many parts of Africa, Asia, and Europe.

- The African wild dog *(Lycaon pictus)* hunts in large packs on the African savanna. It is in danger of extinction.

- The maned wolf *(Chrysocyon brachyurus)* has long legs to enable it to see over the tall grasses of the South American pampas. It is rare but can still be found in Brazil and Argentina.

- The fennec fox *(Vulpes zerda)* is the smallest fox. It lives in the deserts of North Africa, where its large ears act like radiators, sending off heat to help keep it cool.

- The raccoon dog *(Nyctereutes procyonoides)* looks more like a raccoon than a dog! It is found in cold wooded areas of Asia and Europe.

African wild dog

Dogs are very different from wolves. Dogs are tamer and friendlier, and they come in many shapes and sizes. Compared to the wolf, the dog has a smaller brain and smaller teeth for its body size. The wolf lives and hunts in packs that have well-developed social structures.

Some scientists believe dogs are like immature wolves. They think that genetic changes occurred that stopped their mental and physical maturation. This explains why dogs throughout their lives act like wolf youngsters, remaining trusting and playful.

Fennec fox

Many of the new dog traits were useful to early humans. People found that when they bred the fastest dogs together, they produced offspring that were fast dogs. When they bred the toughest dogs together, they produced offspring that were tough dogs, and so on. By the time of the ancient Egyptians, such selective breeding had created strains of swift Greyhound-like dogs that could catch fleeing game, fierce warrior dogs that could fight to the death, and even little lap dogs that could be used like heating pads to soothe aches and pains.

Gray wolf

## Dog Parts

With more than 500 breeds, and all sorts of combinations possible among them, the dog comes in more sizes and shapes than any other species of mammal. That makes describing them tough. Still, every dog can be precisely described if you use some special dog terms. First you need to know what the dog's parts are called. See if you can locate the dewlap, stop, occiput, pastern, withers, croup, and loin on the drawing below. Here's what the dog terms mean:

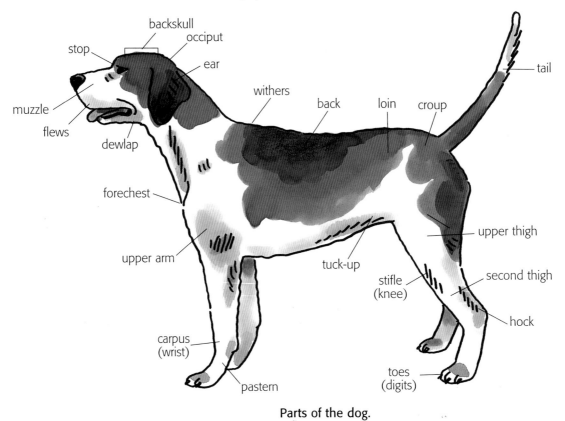

Parts of the dog.

- **Muzzle:** Head in front of eyes, including nasal bone, nostrils, and jaws
- **Stop:** Place between the eyes where the skull starts curving upwards from the muzzle
- **Backskull:** All the parts of the skull from the eyes back
- **Occiput\*:** Point at the very back and top of the head, before it joins the neck

- **Flews:** Hanging upper lips

- **Dewlap:** Loosely hanging skin under the throat

- **Ear:** The part we can see is really the outer ear

- **Withers\*:** Highest part of shoulders, just behind the neck. A dog's height is measured from the floor to the withers

- **Shoulder:** Upper bone (scapula) of front leg assembly

- **Loin:** Area of body on either side of spine between the last ribs and the hind legs

- **Croup\*:** Rearmost part of the back, above the hind legs

- **Upper thigh:** Upper part of hind leg

- **Second thigh:** Lower thigh, corresponding to the human shin and calf

- **Hock joint:** The heel, or rear pastern. The hock is the part of the hind leg between the second thigh and the foot

- **Stifle\*:** Knee joint of hind leg

- **Tuck-up:** Shallower body depth in the loin area

- **Rib cage:** Set of curved bones that extend from the spine on the dog's back to the sternum (breastbone) on the bottom, protecting the heart and lungs

- **Elbow:** Joint of front leg between the upper arm (humerus) and the forearm (radius and ulna)

- **Pastern:** Area of the front leg just below the carpus or wrist

- **Dewclaw:** Toe on the inside of the front leg, and sometimes on the rear leg

- **Upper arm:** Part of the front leg between the elbow and the shoulder

- **Forechest:** Front part of the chest, below the neck

- **Pads:** Shock-absorbing structures beneath the feet, which protect and cushion them.

When we look at the dog's skeleton, we'll learn more about how some of these parts function.

**How to SAY IT**

occiput: OHK-sih-put

withers: WIH-thers

croup: KROOP

stifle: STIE-ful

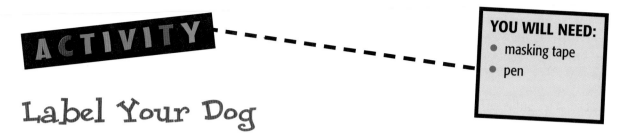

# ACTIVITY

**YOU WILL NEED:**
- masking tape
- pen

## Label Your Dog

Write the name of each part of the dog on a piece of masking tape. Stick each label on your dog in the correct place. The hard part is keeping your dog from pulling them off as fast as you can put them on! Don't go so fast that you scare your dog, and be sure to gently remove the tape when you're finished.

## How Dogs Shape Up

tiny (Chihuahua)    small (Beagle)    medium (Whippet)

large (Labrador Retriever)    giant (Great Dane)

Five sizes of dog: tiny, small, medium, large, and giant.

## From Tiny to Giant

Dogs come in all sizes and shapes. Tiny dogs like Chihuahuas are called toy dogs. Slightly larger dogs like Beagles are called small dogs. Then come medium dogs like Whippets; large dogs like Labrador Retrievers; and finally giant dogs like Saint Bernards. Some breeds are sort of in between, because no definite dividing lines exist between the different sizes. Dogs with long bodies and short legs, like Basset Hounds, are really dwarfed dogs. Dogs' shapes and personalities evolved as they were bred by humans for particular jobs. For example, Basset Hounds, which are low to the ground, were developed for following the scent of rabbits along their trails while hunting. Basset Hounds have short legs so hunters can follow them without needing horses. Their long, dragging ears stir up scents from the ground.

## Tale of the Tails

Dogs vary even down to the tips of their wagging tails!

sabre

ring

curled

gay

plume

Dog tails come in many shapes.

- Tails can be long or short. Short tails have often been docked — that is, shortened at birth. (Docking is illegal in some countries.)
- Tails that are almost missing are called bobtails; short twisted tails are screw tails, and short curled tails are ring tails.
- Tails that hang straight down are sword tails. Tails carried up in the air are gay tails; if they are carried forward over the back they are squirrel tails.
- Medium-length pointed tails are carrot tails; longer tails with a slight curve are sabre tails, and long, straight skinny tails are whip tails.
- Tails with long silky hair on the bottom are plume tails, and tails with fairly long stiff hair are brush tails.

Dogs and other canids communicate with their tails as well as with other body parts (see Body Language). Canids with bushy tails can wrap them around their feet and noses to protect them from the cold.

## Best Foot Forward

stop pad

cat foot

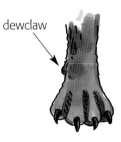

dewclaw

splay foot

**Dog feet come in various shapes.**

Most dogs have cat feet. What? That's a term for round feet. Other dogs have hare feet — long, narrow feet. Dogs have four toes on each rear foot and five on each front foot. Four of the front toes touch the ground. The fifth toe (commonly called the dewclaw) is up on the inside of the front pastern (wrist). A few dogs also have one or even two dewclaws on their rear feet. The extra toes may have helped the tree-climbing ancestors of dogs.

Dog feet have some special features. A dog's claws can't be pulled in (retracted), unlike a cat's claws. This makes dog claws better for digging, which many canids do to make a den, catch an animal that has gone underground, or bury things. Dogs and other canids walk on their toes, which lets them move fast. They don't put their heels down when walking. Dogs have some fused wrist bones, which add strength to their feet. See page 34 for more about feet.

# Would You Believe It?

Dogs come in more sizes and shapes than any other mammal. Here are some examples to show how varied dogs are:

Papillon

French bulldog

Cardigan Welsh Corgi

Doberman

Scottish Deerhound

- **Pug:** toy, level back, ring tail
- **French Bulldog:** small or medium, arched back, screw tail
- **Schipperke:** small, sloping back, bobtail, cat feet
- **Cardigan Welsh Corgi:** medium, dwarf, level back, brush-sabre tail, cat feet
- **Irish Setter:** large, sloping back, plume tail, cat feet

- **Scottish Deerhound:** giant, tucked up, arched back, sabre tail, hare feet
- **Scottish Terrier:** small, level back, gay-carrot tail
- **Siberian Husky:** large, level back, brush-sword tail, cat feet
- **Papillon:** toy, level back, squirrel tail
- **Doberman:** large, level back, docked tail, cat feet

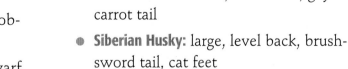

## Guessing Game

Pick a few breeds of dog. Find out about what jobs they were bred to do. What physical and personality traits do they have that help them in their jobs? Pick a few more breeds of dog. Try to guess what their jobs were, based on what you know about their shapes and personalities. Then check some sources to see if you were correct.

moderate (Golden Retriever)     short and wide (Bulldog)     long and narrow (Saluki)

Some dog head shapes.

## Dog Faces

### Head Shapes

Your dog's face is his alone, in the same way that your face is unique, but there is much more variation in the head shapes of dogs than in people's head shapes.

- Dog heads may be round or pointy, rectangular (brick-shaped) or wedge-shaped
- Their skulls can be short and wide, long and narrow, or something in between (moderate)
- Dogs may have flat or rounded backskulls
- The muzzle is the part of the head in front of the eyes, including the nasal bone, nostrils, and jaws. Muzzles can vary in shape, and may be straight, dished (concave), snipy (pointed and weak), or Roman (convex)
- The stop (the step up from muzzle to skull) can be deep or shallow, very noticeable, hardly noticeable, or even arched upward.

We know from fossils that early dogs had moderate-width heads, very similar to those of wolves. Breeding dogs for special purposes resulted in the wide variety of head shapes seen in dogs today.

## Dog Eyes and Ears

### Eye Shapes

Dog eyes can be large or small; deep-set, bulging or drooping; and almond-shaped, round, oval, or triangular. Most dogs have brown eyes, but some have gold eyes and a few have light blue eyes.

triangular

almond-shaped

round

oval

**Eye shapes.**

| prick ears (Malamute) | button ears (Wire-Haired Fox Terrier) | pendant ears (Beagle) |

Ear shapes.

### Ear Shapes

All wild canids and many dogs have ears that stand up, which are called prick ears. Selective breeding has resulted in many different ear shapes in dogs. Prick ears that are broad and round at the tip are called bat ears; ears that fold forward at the top are called semi-prick ears. Ear flaps that fold forward starting near the base to cover the ear opening are called button ears. Ears that fold back are called rose ears. Those that hang down like a Basset Hound's are called pendant ears. Pendant ears can be long, short, rounded, or V-shaped.

At one time, many dogs' ears were surgically cropped to make them upright. Ear cropping has been banned in many countries. The way a dog holds his ears tells things to other dogs about how he is feeling (see Body Language). A dog's sharp sense of hearing helps him locate prey (see Sound Bites).

## SMALLEST AND LARGEST DOG

The smallest adult dog on record, a Yorkshire Terrier named Lanks who lived in the 1940s, supposedly weighed only 4 ounces and stood only 2.5 inches (6 cm) tall at the withers. The smallest recently documented dog was a Chihuahua named Peanuts, who weighed 18 ounces (504 g) and stood 5.5 inches (14 cm) at the withers. The tallest dog on record is a Great Dane named Shangret Danzas, who stood 41.5 inches (105 cm) at the withers.

## That Wonderful Face

Here are just a few of the amazing variety of dog faces:

Boston Terrier

- **French Bulldog:** short, wide skull; round head; pronounced stop; round eyes, bat ears
- **Boston Terrier:** short, wide muzzle; eyes set far apart; short prick ears
- **Collie:** long and narrow triangular head, no stop, flat backskull, triangular eyes, semi-prick ears
- **Chihuahua:** moderate-width round head, pronounced stop, domed backskull, round eyes, prick ears
- **Italian Greyhound:** long and narrow triangular head, slight stop, almond eyes, rose ears
- **Bull Terrier:** moderate-width egg-shaped head, convex stop, triangular eyes, prick ears
- **Fox Terrier:** long, narrow brick head, no stop, deepset round eyes, button ears
- **Rottweiler:** moderate-width round head, pronounced stop, almond eyes, V-shaped pendant ears
- **Irish Setter:** long, narrow brick head; pronounced stop; almond eyes; long pendant ears

Collie

Irish Setter

# Make a Noseprint

**YOU WILL NEED:**
- food coloring
- small pad of paper (memo pad or pad of large self-stick notes)
- paper towels

Did you know that every dog has a noseprint as individual as a person's fingerprint? Test this by collecting dog noseprints. (Read the safety section of the book first.) You've probably seen plenty of dog noseprints on your windows – but here's a way to make a real noseprint.

**1.** Pour some food coloring on a paper towel.

**2.** Dry the dog's nose. Try to keep him from licking his nose after you dry it.

**3.** Gently rub his nose on the paper towel to transfer the coloring. Again, try to keep him from licking his nose!

**4.** Gently press the paper pad to the front of his nose, letting the pad's sides curve around the sides of the nose.

**5.** You want a print where you can see the little patterns on the nose. You will probably have to try several times before it works. If the noseprint is too light, try again with more coloring on the nose. If it's just a big blob, try it again with less coloring on the nose. For good results, keep the dog still and his nose dry! Wash the dog's nose afterward so he doesn't get food coloring all over the place.

Get noseprints from as many different dogs as you can. Do you think they really are as individual as fingerprints?

# The Hair of the Dog

Like all mammals, dogs have hair. Hair is a wonderful thing, because it helps hide and protect the dog. Mammals have two kinds of hair. Dense and soft underhair traps air for insulation, helping to keep the dog warm even in extremely cold and snowy places. The coarser and longer guard hair on the outside protects the dog from being scratched by sticks and thorns. The guard hair colors help to camouflage wild canids, hiding them in their environment. The spotted coloring of the African wild dog is an example of canid camouflage. Some domestic dogs have been bred for unusual hair colors, patterns, or types.

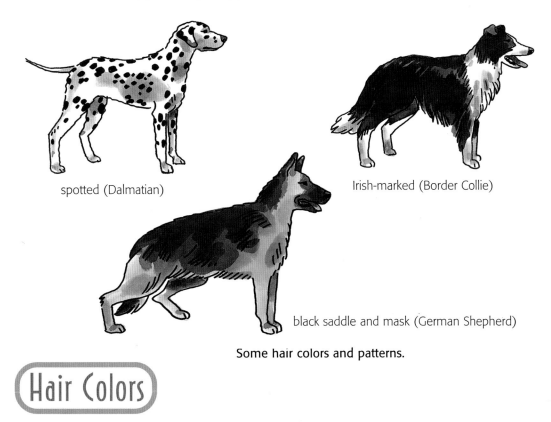

spotted (Dalmatian)

Irish-marked (Border Collie)

black saddle and mask (German Shepherd)

**Some hair colors and patterns.**

## Hair Colors

What color is your dog? That's not always an easy question. Dogs can be solid-colored: black, gray (also called blue); brown, red, gold, cream, or white. Here are some other possibilities:

- **Tan-pointed:** Tan on the muzzle, eyebrows, lower legs, and under the tail. The rest of the body is black, red, or gray.
- **Saddle:** Some dogs have a saddle of dark hair over the back.
- **Agouti\* or domino:** Dark-tipped hairs on the body and light hairs on the legs and face.
- **Sable\*:** Light and dark hairs mingled together.
- **Brindle\*:** Light hair overlaid with darker irregular vertical stripes.
- **Black mask:** A mask of black hair on the face or muzzle.
- **Merle\*:** Mottled patches of light and dark hair. Can be either red merle (brown and tan patches) or blue merle (gray and black patches).
- **Roan:** White hairs mingled with dark hairs.
- **Piebald:** White with large colored patches is called piebald; if the dog is almost all white with just a few spots, it's called extreme piebald.
- **Irish-marked:** The white is only on the tail tip, muzzle, neck, feet, and maybe the lower legs.
- **Ticked:** Lots of small flecks of color.
- **Harlequin\*:** Irregular patches of black on a white background.

Dogs also may have combinations of these colors and patterns.

## Shedding

**How to SAY IT**

agouti: ah-GOO-tee

brindle: BREN-duhl

follicle: FOHL-ik-uhl

harlequin: HAR-lih-kin

merle: MERL

sable: SAY-bull

All dogs shed their hair twice a year, usually in the spring and fall. This allows them to have a thin coat for warm weather and to grow in a new thick coat for cold weather. It's the changing length of daylight that triggers shedding. That's why dogs that live under artificial lighting, as most housedogs do, also shed year-round. In Poodles and other dogs with very curly hair, the shed hair gets tangled in the unshed hair and won't fall out unless it's brushed out. It forms long mats; in some dogs these mats are split apart and form long mop cords that can hang to the ground.

# Straight, Curly, Smooth, or Coarse

What makes hair straight, wavy, or curly? Each hair grows out of a hair follicle,* a tiny hole in the skin. The shape of the hair follicle determines the shape of the hair. Round follicles make round hair shafts, which grow straight. Oval follicles make oval hair shafts, which are wavy, and flat follicles make flat hair shafts, which become curly hair. The same is true for human hair.

Dog hair may be coarse or fine or something in between. Here are some examples: long straight hair (Irish Setter); long coarse hair (Old English Sheepdog); stand-off coat (Akita); both short and long (Saluki); hairless (Chinese Crested); corded (Komondor); short and silky (Whippet); curly (Curly-Coated Retriever); wiry (Airedale).

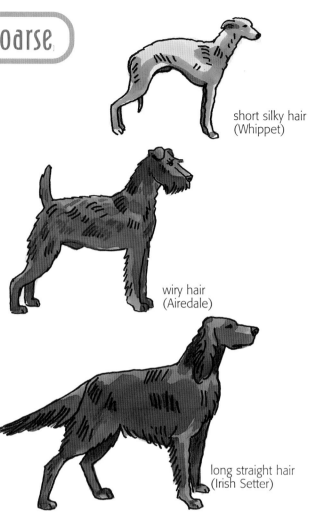

short silky hair (Whippet)

wiry hair (Airedale)

long straight hair (Irish Setter)

Some examples of coat types.

## ACTIVITY

# Identi-Dog: Make a Dog Field Guide

Now that you know all the ways that the parts of dogs can differ, you can use that information to describe each dog you meet, using the Dog I.D. Checklist on the next page. Photocopy it as many times as you need it. If you can, make a sketch to go with it.

Challenge: Get a book of dog breeds or watch a dog show on television and describe every breed using these traits. Can you think of some more traits to add to our list? Here's another activity: Have a friend choose the traits she would like in a dog. Try to find a breed of dog that combines as many of her preferred traits as possible. If no such breed exists, draw the dog she describes.

# Dog I.D. Checklist

| | | | | | |
|---|---|---|---|---|---|
| **SIZE:** | toy | small | medium | large | giant |
| **LEG LENGTH:** | dwarf | average | long | | |
| **BODY:** | heavy | average | light | | |
| **TOPLINE:** | level | sloping | arched | swayed | |
| **UNDERLINE:** | fat | average | tucked-up | | |
| **TAIL:** | | | | | |
| **Length:** | long | medium | docked | bob | |
| **Carriage:** | low | level | gay | | |
| **Shape:** | screw | ring | squirrel | carrot | sabre |
| | whip | straight | | | |
| **Hair on tail:** | smooth | plume | brush | | |
| **FEET:** | cat | hare | flat | splayed | |
| **HEAD:** | | | | | |
| **Shape:** | triangular | broad | round | brick-shaped | |
| **Face:** | pushed in | average | long & narrow | | |
| **Forehead:** | domed | flat | | | |
| **Stop:** | arched | absent | pronounced | | |
| **Muzzle:** | straight | dished | Roman | snipy | deep |
| **EYES:** | | | | | |
| **Set:** | deep-set | average | bulging | | |
| **Size:** | small | average | large | | |
| **Shape:** | round | almond | triangular | | |
| **Lids:** | tight | drooping | | | |
| **Color:** | dark | light | blue | | |
| **EARS:** | | | | | |
| **Shape:** | prick | semi-prick | bat | | |
| | button | rose | drop | | |
| **Size:** | long | short | | | |
| **Color:** | _____ | | | | |
| **COAT:** | | | | | |
| **Length:** | short | medium | long | | |
| **Texture:** | soft | harsh | wiry | | |
| **Type:** | straight | wavy | curly | | |
| **Colors:** | _____ | | | | |
| **SKIN:** | smooth | wrinkled | | | |

**Draw a picture of dog**

**DOG SEEN AT:** _____ on _____ (date)

**BREED OF DOG:** _____

32

# Dog Bones

The skeleton is the framework that supports your dog and allows her to stand and move. Dogs may look different from one another on the outside, but all dogs have the same bones on the inside. The bones just vary in size and shape in different breeds of dog. The adult human skeleton has 206 bones in it. The adult dog skeleton has about 310 bones.

Dog skeletons have some special features, which evolved over millions of years as their carnivore ancestors chased prey across the grasslands:

- Lightweight bones are good for running
- Long legs, with long metacarpals* and metatarsals* are good for speed

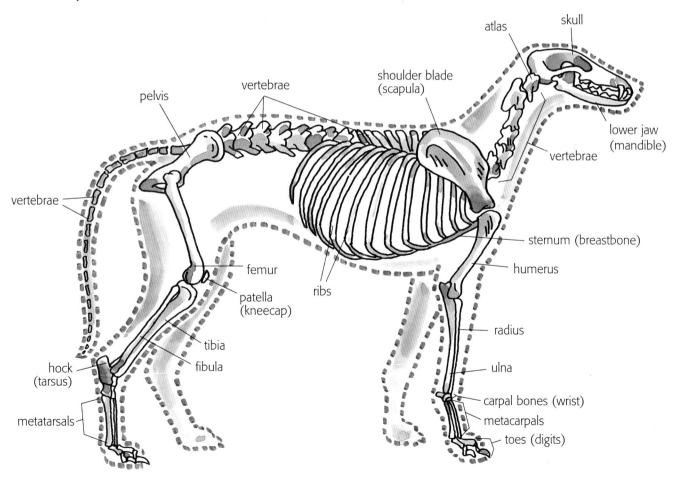

A dog's skeleton.

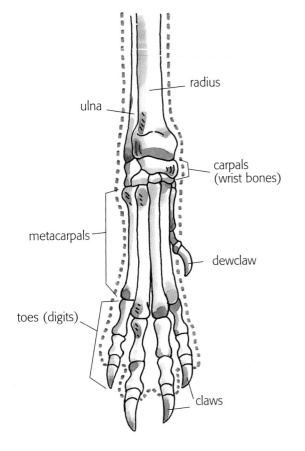

radius

ulna

carpals (wrist bones)

metacarpals

dewclaw

toes (digits)

claws

Bones of the right front foot, seen from the front.

- The shoulder blade can move in line with the front leg. This means the front leg can take bigger strides. The collarbone is very tiny so it doesn't get in the shoulder blade's way

- Fused wrist bones are good for absorbing the shock of landing when running (all carnivores have this trait)

- Thin ulna* bone of front leg fits tightly into a notch in the radius* bone, which prevents rotation of the lower leg when running

- Strong jaws and specialized teeth let canids grip, kill, and eat prey.

Like your bones, dog bones are held together at joints. Joints work in several different ways. Two main types are hinge joints and ball-and-socket joints. Hinge joints, such as the elbow and stifle joints, work like door hinges. They only allow movement back and forth. Ball-and-socket joints, such as the hip joint, work like a joystick in a video game. They allow circular movement. Tendons — tough, flexible tissues that connect muscles to bones — help transmit muscle movements to the bones so the joints will move. Find the same joints in your dog's body and in your own body. Do they move in the same directions?

**How to SAY IT**

carnassials: car-NASS-ee-alls

carpals: CAR-puls

cartilage: KAR-tuh-lij

digits: DIH-jits

femur: FEE-mer

fibula: FIB-u-luh

humerus: HEW-mer-us

incisors: IN-size-ers

mandible: MAN-dih-bul

metacarpals: MET-uh-CAR-puls

metatarsals: MET-uh-TAR-suls

patella: pah-TELL-ah

pelvis: PEL-vis

radius: RAY-dee-us

scapula: SKAP-you-lah

sternum: STUR-num

tarsus: TAR-sus

tibia: TIB-ee-uh

ulna: UHL-nah

vertebrae: VERT-ih-bray

Your dog's skull protects his brain, eyes, ears, and nose. It also houses his teeth — lots of them! The mandible* (lower jaw) opens and closes so he can grasp and chew.

Dogs have several kinds of teeth, each with its own function. The little teeth in the front of the mouth, called incisors,* are good for pulling meat off bones. The big fangs, called canine teeth, are good for grabbing and killing prey. Behind the fangs are the premolars and molars; they are made for serious chewing and crushing. The dog's strong molars can be used to crush bones. Dogs have special teeth called carnassials* — the last upper premolar and the first lower molar — which have sharp tips and high cusps that can cut through flesh. Carnassials are typical teeth of carnivores.

The top and bottom teeth come together in most dogs with the top incisors just in front of the bottom ones. This is called a scissors bite. Most people's teeth come together this way too. In some dogs, the top teeth are so far in front of the bottom ones that a gap is between them; this is an overbite. In other dogs (for example, Bulldogs), the bottom incisors are in front of the top ones; this is an underbite.

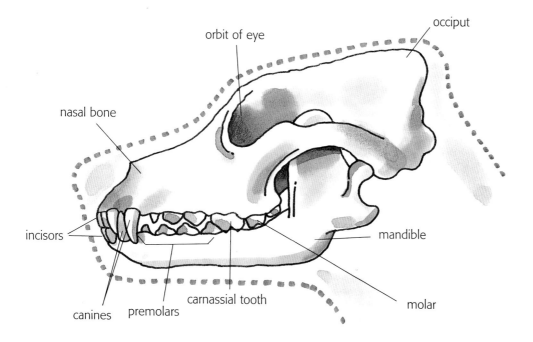

**Dog skull showing teeth closed in scissors bite.**

# Get to Know Your Dog's Skeleton

The dog's backbone is made of many small bones called vertebrae.* The biggest ones are right behind the skull.

1. You can feel the sides of the atlas (the first vertebra, just behind the dog's head) on either side of the neck. The vertebrae protect the spinal cord, an important bundle of nerves that connects the brain to the rest of the body. The backbone also helps the dog move by transmitting power from the rear legs to push the dog forward. Soft discs are found between the vertebrae; they are made of cartilage,* an elastic tissue that provides a cushion between bones.

2. Carefully feel all the way down your dog's back; can you feel the top parts of her vertebrae? The last parts of the backbone are the bones of the tail; they're easy to feel!

3. Feel the way that the ribs circle the dog's chest from her backbone to her sternum.* They protect her heart and lungs, and also help her breathe. Muscles between the ribs contract to make the rib cage smaller and force air out of the lungs; then they relax so the rib cage expands, pulling air into the lungs.

4. The bones of the legs and feet are specialized for holding the dog up and for moving her in different directions. Unlike people, dogs walk on their toes. You can feel this as you move your hand down the dog's hind leg. Check out the way the joints of your feet move, compared to your dog's feet. You have the same bones and joints, but your dog stands on the balls of her feet. The heels do not touch the ground. On the dog's front feet, the situation is the same — only the toes touch the ground.

5. You can feel the top of your dog's shoulder blade, or scapula,* at her withers. Unlike you, the dog doesn't have a large collarbone.

6. Follow the shoulder blade down toward her forechest. The shoulder blade ends in a joint that connects it to the humerus* (upper bone of the front leg), which you can feel slanting downward and rearward toward the elbow.

7. Can you feel the other bones of the front leg? Try feeling the tiny carpal* bones of the wrist. Move your hand downwards to feel the metacarpals. Then feel the toes. How do the bones of the toes compare to your finger bones?

8. On your dog's back, you should be able to feel two bony bumps on either side near the top of the croup. These hipbones are part of the pelvis.*

9. Now feel your dog's stifles (knees), found on the hind legs. If you are very careful, you can feel a tiny oval-shaped bone right in front of the joint. That's the patella* (kneecap).

10. Follow the big bone of the hind leg upward. That's the femur.* It connects to the pelvis in a special ball-and-socket joint.

11. Going back to the stifle (knee), follow the larger bone (tibia*) down toward the hock (ankle joint). Just behind the tibia and above the hock is a thin area that seems like it's just skin; it's like the thin area on your leg just above your heel. Behind this thin area is a huge tendon called the Achilles* tendon; it helps move the foot.

*See page 34 for How to Say It.

# Muscles

Dogs have many muscles. There are three different muscle types: smooth, cardiac, and skeletal. Smooth muscles line the internal organs; for example, they are responsible for stomach contractions. Cardiac muscles are found only in the heart; their contractions produce the heart's beats. Skeletal muscles usually are attached to one end of a bone and then stretch across a joint to attach to part of another bone. Skeletal muscles let the dog move in one direction or the other simply by contracting (getting smaller) and relaxing.

Muscles can only pull bones by contracting; they can't push bones. Muscles usually work in pairs; one muscle group contracts while an opposing muscle group relaxes in order to pull a bone in one direction. For the bone to move back to where it started, the two muscle groups must change roles — the first group relaxes and the second one contracts. Muscles attach to bones by tendons.

Some muscles, especially those on the face, attach to the skin. They control facial expressions by contracting and relaxing in different combinations.

You can feel many of these muscles when you pet your dog.

Like other carnivores, the dog has very strong jaw-closing muscles (temporalis muscles), which served the dog's ancestors to capture and hold prey even when the jaws weren't closed. The masseter muscle supplies the force to cut flesh.

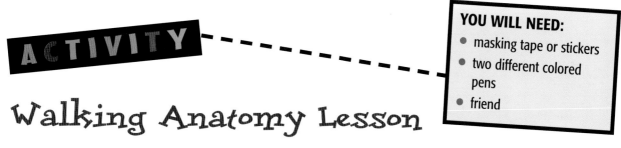

**ACTIVITY**

**YOU WILL NEED:**
- masking tape or stickers
- two different colored pens
- friend

## Walking Anatomy Lesson

You can label your dog's bones the same way you labeled her external parts. Write the name of each bone on some masking tape or on a sticker. Stick them on your dog in the correct places. Now make two sets of stickers; every time you place one on the dog, place the one corresponding to the same bone on yourself or on a friend.

# Heart to Heart

All the cells in your dog's body depend on oxygen to survive. Blood, pumped by the heart and carried through the tube-shaped blood vessels, carries oxygen to the cells. Blood does more than carry oxygen, though. It carries vitamins and other nutrients to cells throughout the body. It also carries hormones that control growth and many other body functions. Blood cells also fight infections. Finally, blood helps regulate body temperature by moving heat from the body's hot interior to the body's colder outer regions. Here's how the circulatory system works:

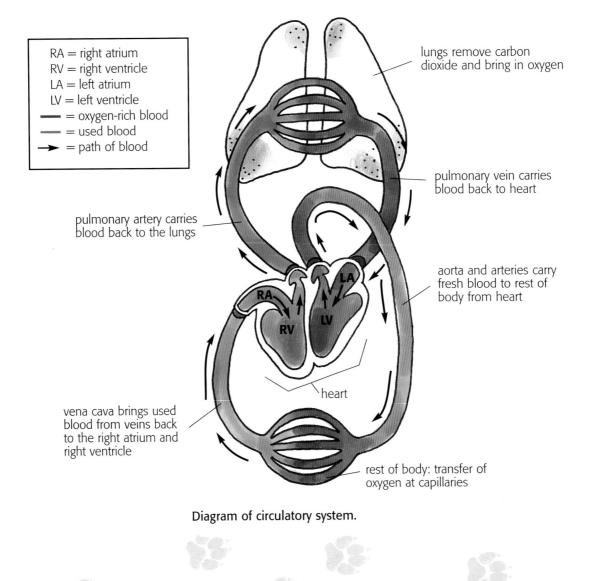

RA = right atrium
RV = right ventricle
LA = left atrium
LV = left ventricle
▬▬ = oxygen-rich blood
▬▬ = used blood
➤ = path of blood

lungs remove carbon dioxide and bring in oxygen

pulmonary vein carries blood back to heart

pulmonary artery carries blood back to the lungs

aorta and arteries carry fresh blood to rest of body from heart

vena cava brings used blood from veins back to the right atrium and right ventricle

heart

rest of body: transfer of oxygen at capillaries

Diagram of circulatory system.

- The heart beats to pump blood

- Blood leaves the left ventricle* (chamber) of the heart

- Arteries,* which are muscular blood vessels, carry the fresh blood throughout the body. The pulse, the rhythmical throbbing felt as the heart pumps blood through an artery, can be easily felt in the dog's femoral* artery

- Arteries divide into smaller and smaller blood vessels, ending in tiny blood vessels called capillaries,* where the transfer of oxygen to cells occurs

- Used blood travels from capillaries to other blood vessels called veins, which carry it back to the heart

- Blood enters the right atrium* (chamber) of the heart and then flows to the right ventricle

- Blood is pumped from the right ventricle through the pulmonary* arteries to the lungs

- Lungs remove carbon dioxide, the gas produced when the cells use oxygen, from blood and replace it with oxygen from inhaled air

- Oxygen-rich blood returns to the left atrium of the heart by way of the pulmonary veins

- Blood is pumped from the left atrium to the left ventricle and the cycle continues.

**SAY IT**

**atrium:** A-tree-um

**arteries:** ART-er-ees

**capillaries:** KAP-eh-lair-ees

**femoral:** FEE-mor-al

**pulmonary:** PUL-mon-AIR-ee

**ventricle:** VEN-trik-al

## ACTIVITY

# Keep Your Finger on the Pulse

1. You can feel your dog's heartbeat by placing your fingertips on her rib cage just behind her left elbow. The exact spot will depend on how your dog is built, so you'll need to feel around some.

2. You can also hear the heartbeat by placing your ear on her chest in the same area.

3. You can even feel the blood pulse through the femoral artery. Place your hand around the upper part of your dog's thigh so your thumb is on the outside and your fingertips are on the inside. Gently feel around for a pulse; the femoral artery is inside the upper rear leg, almost where the leg and the abdomen are joined.

4. Count the number of heartbeats or pulses per minute. How does your dog's heart rate compare to your own heart rate? If you can find several dogs, see if the dog's body size and heart rate are related. How does exercise affect heart rate?

5. You can see the blood circulating in your dog's body by looking at her gums. The gums should be pink, because of the blood in tiny capillaries just below the surface. If you press on the gums with your thumb, you will squeeze the blood out of the area and leave a white thumbprint for just a second. Then the blood will flow back and the area will be pink again. This is one way a veterinarian checks to see if the dog's circulation is working correctly. If the gums are the wrong color to start with, or if they take more than a couple of seconds to turn pink again, the dog may have a heart or blood problem.

## Take a Deep Breath

Oxygen gets inside your dog's body through her lungs. But she has to actively suck it in and push it out to get enough oxygen flow to satisfy her oxygen-hungry cells. To do this, the muscles between her ribs, as well as the diaphragm* — a large sheet of muscles between the lungs and abdomen — work together to expand and contract the rib cage, pulling air into and pushing air out of the lungs.

- Air enters through nostrils at the end of the nose
- The mucus-lined nasal passages trap dust as well as moistening and warming incoming air
- The mouth lets even more air in and out for faster breathing during exercise

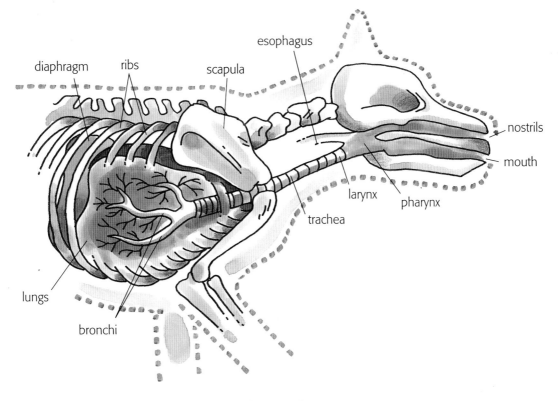

How a dog breathes.

- The pharynx* connects the nose and mouth to the trachea
- The trachea,* or windpipe, leads to the lungs
- The larynx* vibrates when air rushes past it, producing sounds
- The bronchi* are the main tubes leading from the trachea. One goes to each lung
- The two lungs are made up of separate segments called lobes
- The alveoli* are tiny air sacs in the lungs where the gases diffuse in and out of tiny blood vessels
- The pulmonary arteries bring low-oxygen blood to the lungs
- The pulmonary veins take high-oxygen blood to the heart
- The ribs protect the lungs and other organs
- The intercostal* muscles between the ribs help the lungs expand and contract.

Puppies and small dogs breathe more rapidly than large or adult dogs do. Medium-sized adult dogs typically breathe about 10 to 30 times each minute. Ill dogs may also breathe faster, especially those with heart problems.

## SAY IT

alveoli: al-VEE-oh-lye

bronchi: BRON-ki

diaphragm: DIE-ah-fram

intercostal: IN-ter-COHST-al

larynx: LARE-ingks

pharynx: FARE-ingks

trachea: TRAY-kee-ah

## Woof!

Inhaled and exhaled air rushes past the larynx, or voice box. The larynx is bordered by two thin sheets of tissue called vocal cords, which can be closed to form a gap of various sizes. Unless they're all the way open, air rushing past them makes them vibrate, which in turn makes all the different barks, growls, howls, and whines your dog makes.

Gently place your fingers on the outside of your dog's throat when he barks or whines. Can you feel the different vibrations?

## Coughing, Choking, and Yawning

The body has many mechanisms to keep dirt out of its lungs. One way is to forcefully blow it out. That's what happens when your dog sneezes or coughs.

- Sneezing occurs when something tickles the lining of the nose. Coughing occurs when something tickles the lining of the trachea or lungs.

## ACTIVITY

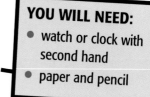

**YOU WILL NEED:**
- watch or clock with second hand
- paper and pencil

## Breathing Rate

Record your dog's breathing rate for one minute when she is at rest and when she is exercising. How much time after exercising does it take for her breathing rate to return to its resting rate?

## ACTIVITY

**YOU WILL NEED:**
- human helper
- watch or clock with second hand
- paper and pencil

# Ho-Hum

Have you noticed that yawns are contagious? Nobody really knows why. Even talking about yawning can make you yawn. (Are you yawning now?) Try this experiment:

1. Observe another person for one minute and record how many times she yawns. Don't let her know what you're doing!

2. Now yawn in front of the person; try to make it look natural. Watch the person for another minute and record how many times she yawns.

3. Next, repeat steps 1 and 2, but with your dog.

Record your dog's yawning for one minute; then yawn in front of him and record his yawns for another minute. Is yawning more contagious between species or within the same species? Can dogs "catch" yawns from people?

4. Now wait until your dog yawns in front of a person. Observe what happens. Can people "catch" yawns from dogs?

5. If you have more than one dog, you can also do the experiment to see if dogs can "catch" yawns from other dogs.

- Choking occurs when something is blocking the airway. The dog will try to expel the item by coughing or gagging, but sometimes she can't. A small ball can be just the right size to plug up a dog's airway and choke her. Sometimes a dog accidentally sucks a ball into her airway while playing. If your dog has a ball or any toy that's small enough to swallow, it's too small for her to be playing with. She could choke.

- Yawning is a way of getting an extra burst of oxygen into the lungs. Like people, dogs get bored, and when they do, their breathing can become slow and shallow — sometimes to the point that their bodies aren't getting enough oxygen. Try yawning and notice how you inhale deeply in the process.

# A Bundle of Nerves

Your dog's nervous system is the part that lets her think, feel, and move. The nervous system is made up of billions of special cells called neurons,* which are grouped together to form the brain and nerves. The nerves form an information network all over the dog's body, receiving input from the outside world through special neurons called receptors, then zipping a message to the spinal cord or brain at superfast speeds (from 3 to 300 feet per second, or 1 to 92 m per sec), getting a decision from the brain, and finally zipping an answer back to the muscles, telling them what to do.

The nervous system has two main parts: the central nervous system and the peripheral* (outer) nervous system. The central nervous system is made of the brain and the spinal cord. The peripheral nervous system carries messages between the central nervous system and the rest of the body. It communicates with the brain by way of pairs of nerves that leave the spinal cord in the spaces between the vertebrae.

## Headquarters

The brain is the headquarters of the nervous system. Its size depends on how big the dog is, but even the biggest dog brain can't come close to your brain, which weighs almost 1400 grams (3 pounds). For example, a Beagle's brain weighs only 72 grams (less than 3 ounces). Even the brain of a Saint Bernard weighs only about 15 percent of your brain's weight. The brain is divided in two halves, called hemispheres. The right half controls the left side of the body, and the left half controls the right side of the body. Why dogs, people, and other animals evolved this way, nobody knows at present.

- The cerebral cortex* is the outer covering of the top of the brain. Smarter animals have more cerebral cortex, so it has to be crinkled up to wrap around the brain — like wrapping a ball with a big piece of paper. That's why the surface of the brain looks all folded and wrinkled. Different parts of the cortex are specialized for different jobs:

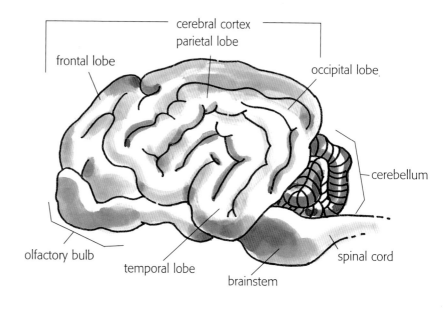

The dog's brain.

- ◆ The frontal lobe is where the dog thinks and makes decisions
- ◆ The parietal* lobe is where the dog gets information about touch
- ◆ The temporal* lobe is where the dog interprets sounds, including dog barks and people talk
- ◆ The occipital* lobe is where the dog interprets what he sees

- The cranial* nerves bypass the spinal cord to take messages to and from the eyes, mouth, ears, nose and head, as well as to and from some internal organs

- The olfactory* bulb is the part of the brain your dog uses to understand smells. It's very large in dogs, who have a very good sense of smell. In people, the olfactory lobe is only about the size of a pencil eraser

- The cerebellum* controls balance, coordination, and learned movements. It allows your dog to run, jump, and even catch a ball without falling. It also stores memories of complicated movements. Once your dog learns to catch a ball, the sequence of movements needed to do so is ready for the next time

- The brainstem controls basic functions, like breathing and maintaining heart rate

- The spinal cord carries information to the rest of the body; it runs almost all the way down the back, protected by the vertebrae.

# How to SAY IT

abducens: ab-DU-sins

accessory: ack-SESS-or-ee

cerebrum: se-REE-brum

cerebellum: SER-eh-BELL-um

cerebral cortex:
se-REE-bral KOR-tecks

cranial: KRAY-nee-al

glossopharyngeal:
GLAHS-oh-far-IN-jee-al

hypoglossal:
HIGH-po-GLAHS-al

neuron: NOO-ron

occipital: AHK-sip-it-al

oculomotor:
AH-kew-low-moe-tor

olfactory: ol-FAK-tor-ee

optic: OP-tik

parietal: pa-RY-it-al

peripheral: peh-RIF-er-al

temporal: TEMP-or-al

trigeminal: try-JEM-in-al

trochlear: TROE-klee-ar

vagus: VAY-gus

vestibulocochlear:
ves-TIB-u-lo-KO-klee-ar

vibrissae: vie-BRISS-ae

# LIVE AND LEARN

When a puppy is born, his brain has billions of neurons. As the puppy grows and learns, the brain doesn't add more neurons, but it does add more connections between neurons. A puppy who grows up in a boring environment with nothing to investigate, play with, or learn will never develop as many connections between neurons as a puppy who grows up in a stimulating environment.

46

# ACTIVITY

# Test Your Dog's Cranial Nerves

Your dog has 12 cranial nerves, each with a different function. You can test your dog to make sure hers are all working as they should be. You have the same cranial nerves as your dog, so you can take the same test!

## Olfactory Nerve

The olfactory nerve connects the nose to the brain. To test it you will need:
- paper towel
- good-smelling treat, like cheese or meat

Cover the treat with the paper towel and place it in front of your dog. She should sniff the towel and find the treat.

## Optic Nerve

The optic* nerve connects the eyes to the brain. To test it you will need:
- window or glass door
- helper

Let your dog look through the window and have your helper appear. Your helper can hold up a leash or do anything but make noise to get your dog's attention. Your dog should respond.

## Oculomotor, Trochlear, Abducens Nerves

The oculomotor,* trochlear,* and abducens* nerves all control eye movements and pupil diameter. To test them you will need:
- light source
- toy or empty food bowl
- helper

Have your helper hold your dog's head so she looks straight ahead. Take the toy or bowl and move it from

**(Oculomotor, continued)**

side to side and up and down. The dog should move her eyes to follow the object. To check the pupillary response (reaction of her pupils to light), look at the size of her pupils in bright light and in dim light. They should be smaller in bright light.

## Trigeminal Nerve

The trigeminal* nerve transmits many sensations to and from the face, nose, and mouth. To test it you will need:
- cotton swab
- piece of food

To test the sensory function, touch the cotton swab to your dog's mouth and see if she responds in any way. If she's panting, you can touch the swab to her mouth to see if she stops panting for a second. She should show you that she can feel a light touch around her face and mouth.

To test the movement function, give her the food. She should move her jaws to chew it.

## Facial Nerve

The facial nerve controls some facial expressions and some taste responses. To test it you will need:
- treat

Try to get your dog to prick her ears up or change her facial expression by showing her a treat. She should be able to move her ears or make a face.

## Vestibulocochlear Nerve

The vestibulocochlear* nerve connects the ear to the brain. It controls hearing and balance. To test it you will need:
- a way to make noise

**(continued on next page)**

# Test Your Dog's Cranial Nerves
## (continued)

**(Vestibulocochlear, continued)**

Stand behind your dog or somewhere else where your dog can't see you, and call her, yell, or whistle. She should respond to the sound.

## Glossopharyngeal Nerve

The glossopharyngeal* nerve is responsible for taste and touch information from some parts of the tongue; it's also involved in swallowing. To test it you will need:

- cotton swab
- treat

If you dog is panting, touch her tongue with the cotton swab. She should move it or close her mouth for a second. Then give her a treat to eat; she should be able to swallow it.

## Vagus Nerve

The vagus* nerve is important for digestion and regulating heart rate. To test it you will need:

- watch that can measure seconds

Practice counting your dog's heart rate (page 40).

**(Vagus, continued)**

Measure your dog's heart rate while she's resting. Then take her out to play and run. Stop and measure it again; it should be faster.

## Spinal Accessory Nerve

The spinal accessory* nerve controls the muscles used to move the head. To test it you will need:

- treat or toy

Move a treat or toy back and forth and up and down in front of your dog. Your dog should move her head.

## Hypoglossal Nerve

The hypoglossal* nerve controls the muscles of the tongue. To test it you will need:

- bowl of ice water or some crumbs

Give your dog the bowl of water or crumbs. She should use her tongue to lap them up.

*See page 46 for How to Say It.

# See a Reflex in Action

Some simple reactions, called reflexes, are directed by the spinal cord instead of the brain. That way the dog can react very quickly, perhaps picking up his paw if he's stepping on something sharp. Other reflexes are a little more involved. For example, if you scratch your dog on the bottom or side of her chest in a certain place, she'll move her hind leg on that side as though she were scratching herself. See if you can find "the spot" on your dog. You can also see a simple reflex by gently touching your dog's whiskers (actually called vibrissae*) – it will cause her to blink her eyes!

# Your Dog's World

You and your dog may live in the same world, but the ways in which you experience it are very different. You live in a world full of colors that has very few smells. Your dog lives in a world full of rich smells that is less colorful than yours. By asking your dog in the right way, you can find out what she can see, hear, and smell, and even what flavors she likes best. The experiments in this section show you how. Can you expect your dog to understand what you want, even if you don't see the world the same way? You can, as long you understand your dog's point of view. Or is that point of smell?

# A Dog's-Eye View

Many dogs rely on good vision to do their jobs. Dogs in the Greyhound family use their vision to chase game. Guide dogs act as the eyes for sightless people. Retrievers need to see where downed birds have fallen and also must follow the hand signals from the hunter, who may be far away. Dogs see a different world from the one we see. Compared to people, dogs have:

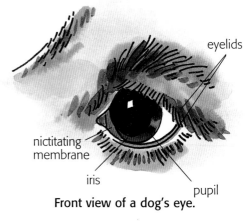

**Front view of a dog's eye.**

- a wider field of view
- poorer detail vision and poorer color vision
- better ability to see in dim light
- better ability to see movement.

Your dog's eyes are like yours, but with a few differences:

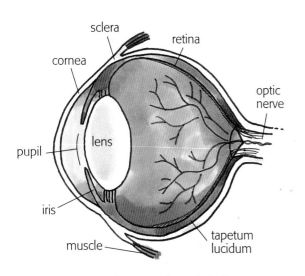

**Cross-section of dog's eye.**

- The eyelids protect the eye from injury, excessive light, and from drying out. Dogs don't blink as often as people do, but the dog has a third eyelid called the nictitating* membrane, a translucent lid that sweeps across the eye from the eye's inner corner, moistening the eye while still letting light through.

- The pupil is the opening through which light enters the eye. The pupil opens more in dim light and closes more in bright light. Compared to people, dogs have larger pupils, which let more light into the eye and help dogs see in dim light. This ability helped the canid ancestors of dogs, who hunted in the evening and at night.

- The iris is a ring of colored muscles that controls the size of the pupil.

- The sclera (white) of the eye is a coat of fibrous tissue that covers and protects the entire eyeball except the cornea.

- The cornea* is the clear-domed covering over the front of the eye. Look at your dog's eye from the side, and you will see it.

A dog's eyes glow in the dark.

- The lens focuses the image of what the dog is looking at on the retina at the back of the eye. Dogs have larger lenses than people do, helping them to see better in dim light.

- The retina* is made up of special cells called rods and cones, which react to light. Rods are very sensitive to dim light but aren't good at seeing details or colors; that's the cones' job. Dog retinas have many more rods than cones, especially compared to retinas of people.

- The tapetum lucidum* is a light-reflective layer that bounces light back.

- Signals from the rods and cones travel to the optic nerve and then to several centers in the brain that process visual information.

## ACTIVITY

**YOU WILL NEED:**
- dark room or yard
- flashlight
- camera with flash (optional)
- friend (optional)

# Make Your Dog's Eyes Glow

The dog has a surprise hidden behind the retina: a shiny layer called the tapetum lucidum. The tapetum lucidum is like a mirror; it reflects light that got past the receptors right back into them for a second chance to be seen. As a result, dogs' eyes will glow if you shine a bright light in their eyes at night.

1. Let your dog stay in the dark for about five minutes so her pupils will get big (open up).

2. Stand about 20 feet (6 m) away, and get her to look at you.

3. Stand right behind the flashlight and shine the light toward her eyes.

4. What color is reflected from your dog's eyes?

5. Take a picture of your dog and of a human friend in dim light, using a camera with a flash. How do their eyes compare in the photographs?

## Loss of Vision

Some dogs lose their vision. This is common when dogs get older. A dog that can't see well may act more timid, dependent, and quiet. He may also have a hard time chasing balls, going down stairs, running or jumping.

Blind dogs can live full lives. They learn where furniture is and can run around the house as long as the furniture isn't moved. They can also be guided by sound and scent. Radios, ticking clocks, wind chimes, perfumed fabrics, carpet runners, and gravel walkways can guide them around the house and yard.

**ACTIVITY**

**YOU WILL NEED:**
- cotton ball
- dim room with movable objects
- penlight or small, bright flashlight
- pillows or chairs in room

# Test Your Dog's Vision

### Pupillary Reflex

**1.** Let your dog's eyes adapt to the dark for about five minutes. This will give her pupils time to get big (open up).

**2.** Still in the dark room, shine the beam from your light at one of your dog's eyes. You may have to flick your light on and off to see the pupil's response better. The pupils of both eyes should get smaller.

### Visual Placing Reflex

If you have a small dog that you can pick up, you can do this test: Hold your dog in your arms facing forward and walk toward a table or bed. Dogs with normal vision will reach forward with their front feet and try to place them on the raised surface as they see it approaching.

### Cotton Ball Test

An easy test is to throw a cotton ball and see if your dog follows it with his eyes. A cotton ball is used because it doesn't make any noise when it hits the ground.

### Obstacle Test

Take your dog to a room he's not used to, or rearrange some of the furniture in one room. Use only soft pillows, chairs, and things that won't hurt your dog if he bumps into them. Then let your dog loose in the room and call him from one side to the other. A dog with normal vision should not bump into any objects. If you suspect your dog isn't seeing well, you might want to see a veterinarian who specializes in diseases of animal eyes.

## In Living Color?

Mammals that ate a lot of fruits and berries over millions of years of evolution usually have good color vision. They needed good color vision to spot ripe fruit. As dogs evolved, they ate mostly meat. Do dogs have color vision? Scientists wondered for years before they solved the mystery. Part of the answer was found in the dog's retina.

Dogs have special light-sensitive cells called cones, which are needed for color vision. However, dogs don't have as many cones, or as many types of cones, as people do. Dogs see greenish-blue colors as white or gray. They can tell the difference between blues and reds, but confuse colors ranging between greenish-yellow and red. Dogs may have a hard time spotting a red ball on a green lawn, for example.

**How to SAY IT**

**cornea:** KORN-ee-ah

**nictitating:** NIK-ti-tate-ing

**retina:** RET-en-ah

**tapetum lucidum:** tah-PEET-um LOO-see-dum

## Smelly Dogs

Take a sniff. You may smell food cooking, maybe your dirty tennis shoes — maybe even your wet dog. But your dog can take a sniff and identify who has walked through the room in the last day, every ingredient in what's cooking, and where your dirty tennis shoes have been. A dog's sense of smell is so much better than ours that it's hard to imagine how rich the dog's world of odors must be.

For the dog's canid ancestors, hunting prey in the evening and at night, a keen sense of smell was very important. This is true for wolves today. Being able to sniff urine markings that other wolves leave lets the wolves avoid other wolf packs in the border areas of their territories, which minimizes disputes and ensures survival.

Dogs have been trained to use their noses to hunt game birds and mammals and to find escaped criminals, lost children, buried disaster victims, illegal drugs and explosives, and even hidden termites. They may even be able to sniff out skin cancer in people and detect oncoming seizures.

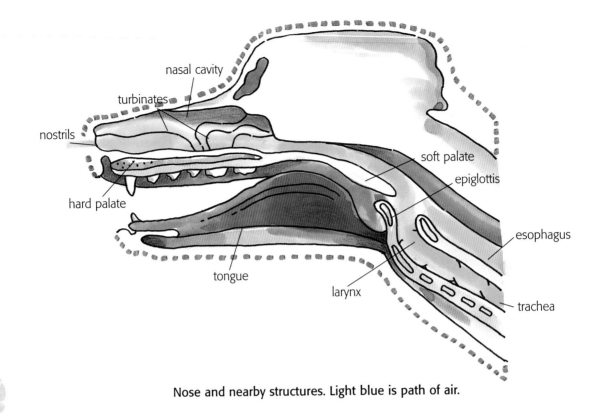

**Nose and nearby structures. Light blue is path of air.**

nasal cavity

turbinates

nostrils

hard palate

tongue

soft palate

epiglottis

esophagus

larynx

trachea

## ( A Guided Tour of Rover's Nose )

To understand why the olfactory (smell) sense of dogs is so much better than ours, take a look inside a dog's nose.

- The nostrils (nares*) are openings that let odors enter the nose
- Connecting to the nostrils, two nasal cavities (spaces) run the length of the muzzle
- Very thin, curved bones called turbinates* create a maze of passageways inside the nasal cavities
- The sides of the nasal passageways are covered by a layer of cells called olfactory epithelium* and mucus. The olfactory epithelium has receptors that poke their tips up through the mucus. Different substances in odors cause different olfactory receptors to signal with a nerve impulse

- The olfactory nerves carry the nerve signals from the olfactory receptors to the brain's olfactory bulb

- The olfactory bulb interprets the various signals and sends messages to the rest of the brain, telling it of the scents. The olfactory bulb is much larger in dogs than it is in most mammals.

One reason dogs have such a great sense of smell is that they have big noses. The larger the dog's muzzle, the more olfactory epithelium he has. A German Shepherd has an olfactory area of 170 square centimeters, a Pekingese has 20 square centimeters, but a person has only 4 square centimeters. The bigger the area of olfactory epithelium, the more olfactory receptors it has. A German Shepherd has 220,000,000 olfactory receptors, a Dachshund has 125,000,000, and a person only has 6,000,000. The more receptors, the more chance of smelling something!

The more receptors, the larger the area of the brain devoted to understanding them. The olfactory bulb of the human brain is tiny, but the olfactory bulb of the dog makes up a large part of his brain.

## How to SAY IT

**epithelium:** ehp-eh-THEE-lee-um

**nares:** NAR-ees

**pheromones:** FER-uh-monz

**turbinates:** TER-ben-ates

**vomeronasal:** VOM-er-oh-NAY-zal

# Hide and Seek

Here's a fun game that almost any dog will love! When you're through, your dog will have learned to use his nose to find tasty treats you've hidden.

1. Show your dog the treat.

2. Let him see you hide the treat. You can hide it under a chair, in a plastic cup, or in long grass.

3. Say "Find it!" and let him go find the treat right away.

4. Once he's found it, he gets to eat it.

5. Repeat this, hiding the treat in slightly more hidden locations each time.

6. Now comes the hard part: Once he understands the game, hide the treat but don't let him watch you hide it.

7. Say "Find it!" as usual and let him look for it. If he's having a hard time, you can guide him to the general area and give him a few hints.

8. As he gets better at using his nose, you can hide the treat in much harder places for your dog to find.

9. Remember to quit the game before he gets bored, and always let him find the treat on the last try before you quit — even if you have to make it easy.

Record your dog's progress. How many treats did you hide? How many could your dog find? Did he begin to find them more quickly with more practice?

What about you? Can you use your nose to sniff out a treat? Set up an experiment to find out.

## Sniffing versus Breathing

When your dog inhales normally, most of the air bypasses the maze of turbinates and goes directly to the trachea and then to the lungs. When your dog wants to smell something, he sniffs in a series of short, shallow breaths, which directs the incoming air into the turbinates, which are covered by the olfactory epithelium. To detect faint odors, your dog will usually sniff more rapidly rather than more deeply. Watch your dog sniff something. Now sniff something yourself. Do you do the same thing?

## Follow Your Nose

How does a dog follow a human scent trail? The dog is the scenting champion of the world. Dogs can smell about 100,000,000 times better than any human. They're even better than machines. They're the only way we have of following scent trails.

The Bloodhound is recognized as the master trailer of the world. His long ears may stir up ground scents and his folds of skin may trap them around his face, helping him to trail. His wet nose, like that of other dogs, attracts and holds odors, which dissolve and are carried inside to be sniffed and recognized by the dog's brain. Dogs have followed human trails that were laid more than 100 hours earlier, and have followed them for up to 135 miles (216 km).

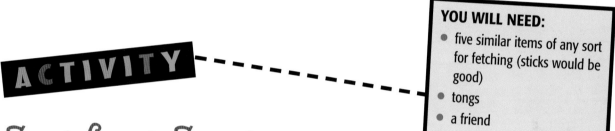

**ACTIVITY**

**YOU WILL NEED:**
- five similar items of any sort for fetching (sticks would be good)
- tongs
- a friend

## Sent for a Scent

1. Choose one of the items and place a tiny mark on it so you can tell it from the others. This is the item you will handle.

2. Teach your dog to retrieve your item. Rub the item in your hands and throw it. Say "Find mine!" and encourage your dog to pick it up. Praise him when he does and give him a treat.

3. Place the other items on the floor or ground using the tongs so you don't get your scent on them. Or ask a friend to place them.

4. Throw your scented item next to them and say "Find mine!" Let your dog watch it land. He should pick it up and bring it to you. Praise him if he does! If he picks up the wrong item, put it away and direct him to the right one.

5. Once your dog is good at that, let him see you throw the item but don't let him see it land. He will have to use his nose to figure out which one you threw!

6. You can make it even harder by setting the item among the others when he isn't looking. Then tell him to "Find mine!" and see if he can sniff it out!

**ACTIVITY**

# Hot on Your Trail?

Have you ever wondered how they train Bloodhounds to track lost people? You can train your dog the same way. One way is to teach your dog that he can find treats along your scent trail.

1. Walk in a straight line for about 20 feet (6 m). Drop a small dog treat every few feet — sort of like leaving a trail of breadcrumbs. Place a bigger pile of treats at the end of the trail.

2. Retrace your steps to where your dog is.

3. Say "Track!" and point to the ground where your trail is. You may have to help direct your dog from treat to treat at first.

4. Repeat this, but gradually walk for a longer distance and leave a bigger space between the dropped treats. Be sure you either retrace your exact tracks from the first time or use a totally new part of the field.

5. Don't be discouraged; it often takes a long time before dogs realize they can find the treats by following your scent trail.

6. When your dog can find the treats when they are 15 feet (4.5 m) apart, add a right angle turn to your track.

7. Eventually you can drop fewer and fewer treats, and add more turns and distance. You can even hide at the end of the trail and have your dog find you. Be sure to have lots of treats and praise ready for your dog when he tracks you down!

You can record your dog's progress. How long was the trail you laid? How far apart were the treats? How many treats could your dog find without help? How long did it take for your dog to reach the last pile of treats at the end of the trail?

# Tongues Are Wagging!

Can you think of some foods you like that your dog doesn't like? Or some foods that your dog likes but you don't? The tongue acts as a gatekeeper to the stomach, seeking some foods while keeping others out, depending on their taste. Different species have inborn taste preferences that are related to their special nutritional requirements.

The dog's tongue is a strong and flexible muscle that is used to lap up liquids and help move food around in the mouth. The tongue is also where the sense of taste occurs.

Here's how a tongue works:

- Papillae* are small bumps on the tongue. Each papilla contains clusters of taste buds. Each taste bud in turn contains about 50 taste receptor cells

- Taste buds in different areas of the tongue respond to different taste (or flavor) molecules.* These taste buds are in various different areas of the tongue. For example, in people, the tip of the tongue is most sensitive to sweet, but in dogs, the rear of the tongue is more sensitive to sweet

- Compared to people, dogs can't taste salt very well, although they still taste it well enough to enjoy it

- A dog's tongue also is very important in helping her cool off (see Hot Dogs, page 86).

# Food Preferences

Deciding what a dog likes to eat may seem like an easy task. Place a bowl of food in front of the dog and see if she eats it. Place a bowl of a different food in front of her the next day and see if she eats more or less of it. But what if the dog is starving and would eat anything? What if she is sick and won't eat anything? Differences in a food's nutritional and calorie content may influence how much she eats before feeling full; some foods are very filling and some are not.

Another way to test preferences is to give her two types of food at once and see which she eats first or most of. Of course some dogs keep eating out of whatever bowl their nose is in, and some dogs lick both bowls clean, no matter how much food you put in them! Asking a dog what she likes to eat is harder than it looks.

## YUM!

Dogs prefer meat to vegetables, and most prefer beef and pork over lamb over chicken. They also generally prefer warm, moist foods more than cold, dry food.

## YUCK!

Can you remember eating something — especially something you had never eaten before — and then getting sick to your stomach? Chances are you can't stand to eat that same food now. The same thing happens for dogs. This is a special type of learning called a conditioned taste aversion; it helps animals avoid foods, like poisons, that make them sick and is very important to animals in the wild.

## How to SAY IT

molecule: MAHL-eh-kewl

papillae: pah-PILL-eye

# ACTIVITY

# Find Fido's Favorite Food

There are several ways to do this experiment, so feel free to try your own improvements. Keep the following in mind:

- Don't do this experiment if you have a dog that guards her food or acts aggressive when eating.

- Some dogs will always choose the larger or the smaller piece of food. You need to make the food choices as nearly equal in size as possible.

- Some dogs will tend to always choose the food on either the right or the left side, so change the position of the food samples. You can see if your dog has a side preference by letting her choose between two samples of the same food for many trials, and seeing if she eats mostly from one side.

- Some dogs will eat the first thing they can reach. Make sure the dog is aware that there are two different foods to choose between – let the dog sniff both choices through a screen.

- Some dogs will assume they can eat everything. If possible, teach the dog she can only have one.

1. Place one small food sample in each bowl.

2. Place the two bowls next to each other with the screen over both of them.

3. Let your dog sniff each sample through the screen. It may be better if a helper holds the dog on a leash to keep her from grabbing the food.

4. Place the dog an equal distance between the two samples and remove the screen.

5. Record which food she eats first.

6. Repeat many times, randomly placing the food choices to the right or left.

7. Once you have found a winner between these two choices, compare the winner with another food brand. Continue to make comparisons until you have ranked your dog's preferences from favorite to least favorite.

# Sound Bites

It's the dead of night. Suddenly your dog jumps up, runs to the window and starts barking. You don't hear a thing, but you know your dog well enough to know something is out there. You know she can hear things you cannot. Sound is one way the dog's wolf ancestors, as well as today's wolves, keep in touch with each other when hunting. Through their howls, squeals, yelps, and barks they can keep in contact over distances up to 5 miles (8 km), letting them travel and hunt as a pack, spread out, and capture their prey. The animals they hunt are often very large — for example, moose, caribou, and deer. Alone a wolf would not be able to successfully catch one. Wild canids also locate small prey, such as moles, by sound.

# A Quick Trip Inside Your Dog's Ear

## How to SAY IT

auditory: AWE-di-tor-ee

cochlea: KOKE-lee-ah

Corti: KORT-ee

incus: INK-us

malleus: MAHL-ee-us

ossicles: AH-sick-els

pinna: PIN-nah

stapes: STAY-peez

tympanic: tim-PAN-ic

- The outer ear or pinna* (the part you see) captures sound waves and funnels them into the ear. Dogs use about 30 sets of muscles to move their pinnae toward a sound, compared to the measly six sets of muscles people have.

- The dog's ear canal makes a sharp turn halfway down. Wax in the canal traps dust and foreign particles so they can't harm the inner parts of the ear.

- The eardrum, or tympanic* membrane, vibrates when sound waves hit it.

- The ossicles* are three tiny bones — the hammer (malleus*), anvil (incus*), and stirrup (stapes*) — that vibrate when the eardrum vibrates and magnify the sound.

- The oval window is a thin membrane that transmits the vibrations of the ossicles to the fluid in the cochlea.*

- The cochlea is a spiral-shaped, fluid-filled structure consisting of three long tubes. When the oval window vibrates, it pushes the end of one of the long tubes, in turn pushing the fluid in the tube to the other end.

- The organ of Corti* is inside the cochlea. It contains thousands of tiny hair-like nerve cells. When the fluid rushes down the cochlea's chambers, it bends the hair cells, causing them to send out nerve impulses.

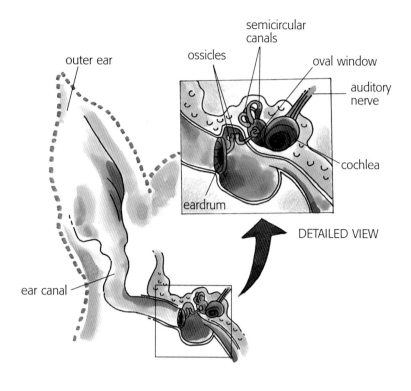

Cross-section of a dog's ear.

- The auditory* nerve carries the nerve impulse to the brain.

- The semi-circular canals are three fluid-filled canals that aren't involved with hearing, but with balance.

Like most animals that evolved to hunt, dogs need to be able to locate where sounds come from. Dogs are much better than people at locating most sounds, especially high-pitched ones. Dogs can hear the high-pitched squeaks of burrowing rodents. Pitch is measured in Hertz (Hz). The lowest-pitched sounds people or dogs can hear are about 50 Hz. People are most sensitive to pitches of about 3000 Hz (close to the pitch of most human voices), while dogs are most sensitive to slightly higher pitched sounds of about 8000 Hz. People can't hear sounds higher in pitch than about 20,000 Hz, but dogs can hear up to 45,000 Hz.

Sounds that are so high-pitched that people can't hear them are called ultrasounds. So-called silent dog whistles produce ultrasounds that dogs, but not people, can hear. Some models of ultrasonic pest devices, which produce high-pitched sounds that rodents, bats, and insects can hear, may be within the hearing range of dogs. If you have a dog whistle or ultrasonic pest device, use it in the hearing test below and see if your dog can hear it.

Deaf dogs cannot hear their owner's calls or approaching danger. They can be hard to train. People who don't realize their dog is deaf sometimes think she's just stupid or stubborn. But you can communicate with a deaf dog by thumping on the floor to get her attention and then using hand signals to tell her what you want. You can blink a flashlight on and off to call her when it's dark. You can even use a radio-controlled vibrating collar to get her attention at a distance. Can you think of any other ways to talk to a deaf dog?

## ACTIVITY

**YOU WILL NEED:**
- quiet room away from other pets (sometimes other pets can respond to sounds and tip your dog off)
- bell or other noisy item, dog whistle, or ultrasonic pest device (optional)

# Hear, Pup! Test Your Dog's Hearing

Does your dog ignore what you say? Have you wondered if she might be deaf? Many dogs are deaf; dogs of certain colors, especially piebalds or merles, and certain breeds (such as Dalmatians, English Setters, and Jack Russell Terriers) are more likely to be deaf in one or both ears. Some other dogs may become deaf from old age, drugs, or exposure to loud noises. Here's a simple hearing test you can do with your dog at home.

**1.** Stand behind your dog and say a word or phrase that she should know, such as her name, or "Want to go out?" or "Ready to eat?" If she responds, she probably can hear. If she doesn't respond, go to the next tests.

**2.** Stand behind your dog and make sure she can't see you out of the corner of her eye, or see your reflection or shadow, and that she can't feel any wind currents or vibrations from you. Clap your hands, ring a bell, or use your ultrasound device or whistle. If she responds, she probably can hear. If not, go to step 3.

**3.** Wait until your dog is panting, and then repeat step 2. Make a noise and see if she quits panting for a moment. Most dogs will quit panting when they hear a strange noise so they can listen better. If your dog responds by stopping her panting for a second, she probably can hear just fine.

If your dog fails all these tests, tell an adult and consider having your veterinarian test her hearing.

# A Touching Experience

Touch. It's part of what makes sharing our lives with our dogs so enjoyable. You enjoy the touch of your dog's nose and the feel of his fur, and he enjoys the caress of your hand and the warmth of your lap. Touch allows your dog to feel where his limbs are, to avoid injury, to seek comfort, and of course, to enjoy being petted.

The sense of touch is actually composed of four types of sensations: pressure, temperature, pain, and proprioception* (sense of where one's own limbs are).

Some parts of your dog's body are much more sensitive than others. For example, the dog's tongue is extremely sensitive. Parts that are more sensitive have more cells devoted to them in the brain's touch centers.

## The Dog's Skin

Beneath your dog's fur lies his largest organ: his skin. The skin has many functions, including housing many of the receptors important for the sense of touch:

- Free nerve endings are closest to the surface. They are sensitive to pain
- Pressure receptors are located deeper in the skin. They respond to objects that push in on the skin
- Cold receptors are also located deeper in the skin. They respond to cold temperatures
- Light touch receptors are closer to the skin surface. They respond to gentle pressure
- Unlike your skin, a dog's skin doesn't have many sweat glands, except on the pads of her feet, and the sweat glands she has don't keep her cool

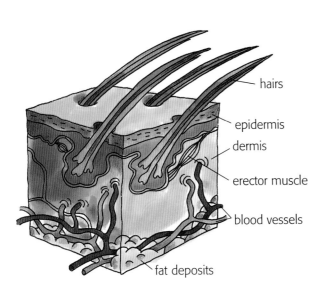

Cross-section of a dog's skin.

- Muscles in the skin can pull the hairs into an upright position
- Top layer or epidermis is thin
- Bottom layer or dermis is thicker and contains many receptors.

## Warm Receptions

In humans, temperature receptors consist of separate nerve endings for hot and cold. In dogs, only cold receptors have been found. This doesn't mean dogs can't feel heat, but that their appreciation of warm things may be achieved in a different way than in humans. In fact, dogs seem not very sensitive to warm items placed on the skin. Their appreciation of a warm spot in the sun may reflect their avoidance of cold rather than a search for warmth. With increased temperature, the dog's pain receptors will eventually respond, so it's possible they can suddenly get the sensation of burning without the warning of increasing warmth.

## Ouch!

Pain has its own receptors, distinct from touch and temperature receptors. Pain makes an animal want to escape from whatever is hurting it, and so can save the animal's life. Animals can't communicate their pain to us in words, and also it may be evolutionarily safer for an animal to hide signs of pain; injured animals quickly can become the targets of predators or other pack members.

You can guess that a dog is in acute pain if he yelps or tries to escape from something, especially if it's something that would also hurt you. Chronic pain is harder to recognize in dogs, but signs include slower movements, lethargy (lack of energy), hiding, loss of appetite, trembling, panting, and irritability.

In general, something that is painful for humans is also painful for dogs. The body has its own built-in pain medicine in the form of substances called endorphins.* These endorphins are released in response to pain; parts of the brain respond to them in a way that dulls the dog's perception of pain. This mechanism probably evolved so that an animal could continue to function as well as possible when it could do no more to avoid pain. Many pain medications work on the same parts of the brain as the endorphins do.

It is far easier to prevent pain than to reduce it once it has grown. Once pain begins, it tends to get worse and be more difficult to stop. Intense pain can cause dogs to recover from injuries more slowly. For these reasons more veterinarians are prescribing pain medication after surgery. Simply because an animal may not communicate that it is in pain does not mean it should have to endure pain.

## Where's My Foot?

The dog uses receptors in his skin and joints to tell him where his limbs are. Like you, he doesn't have to see his leg to know its position. A simple test that a veterinarian might perform to test your dog's proprioception is to

**How to SAY IT**

**endorphins: en-DOR-finz**

**proprioception: PRO-pree-oh-SEP-shun**

pick up one of the dog's feet and place it back down with the top of the foot on the ground. A dog with normal proprioception will immediately move the foot so the foot's pad is on the ground. Try it with your dog.

Get Your Hackles Up

## PUTTING OUT FEELERS

Specialized hairs called vibrissae are present on the dog's face. Although commonly referred to as whiskers, they are unlike the whiskers of humans. They are more rigid and are embedded much more deeply in the skin than other hairs, and they have a greater number of receptor cells at their base. The vibrissae can detect air currents, subtle vibrations, and objects in the dark. They provide an early warning system for objects that might strike the face or eyes. Tap your dog's vibrissae and watch the eye on the same side blink.

Have you ever been so scared you had goose bumps? When dogs get scared or angry, they raise their hackles, the hair around their withers and back, by having goose bumps. Tiny muscles in the skin make each hair stand up. The raised hackles make the dog look larger to his enemies. You can see a hair and skin closeup on page 66.

# Inside Your Dog's Mind

**Y**ou may love how your dog looks, but it's her mind you fell in love with. Her mind sometimes works in mysterious ways. Your dog does a great job of learning about how your mind works; she has to if she's going to get along in a human world! You can meet her halfway. Learn what she's trying to tell you by her behavior and find out how to teach her new things. Have fun getting to know her by giving her an I.Q. test.

# Call of the Wild

The pack of wolves awakens. They stretch, lick each other's faces, and begin to whine. Two males approach each other. One walks with his head held high, while the other crouches and weaves back and forth under the first male's head, licking at his mouth. Like people, wolves and dogs are social animals. Within their group, they tend to form social rankings or hierarchies in which one animal is higher in status, or dominant,* over the lower-status animals. Carefully watching a group of wolves or dogs interact can tell you which one is dominant and which ones are subordinate — as long as you know what their actions mean. There is a dominant male and a dominant female in every wolf pack.

We know about wolf behavior because of the work of scientists called ethologists,* who study the behavior of animals in their natural environments. They try to watch the animals without interfering with their behavior. One of the first things an ethologist does when studying an animal is to make an ethogram,* which is a description of every behavior an animal does. An ethogram for a wolf might include behaviors such as howling, digging, searching, catching prey, chewing and sleeping.

Your dog is a domesticated wolf, and your home is his natural environment. His behaviors that might be included on an ethogram include:

| | | |
|---|---|---|
| Sleeping | Chewing | Holding head high |
| Lying on side | Drinking | Slinking |
| Rolling over | Sniffing another dog | Wagging tail slowly |
| Standing on hind legs | Growling | Wagging tail in circle |
| Sitting | Barking | Tucking tail |
| Walking | Howling | Raising hackles |
| Scratching | Whining | Chasing |
| Shaking off water | Curling up lip | Biting |
| Trembling | Squinting eyes | Rubbing |
| Urinating | Folding ears down | Leaning |
| | Yawning | Carrying |

# Make an Ethogram

You can make your own ethogram by watching your dog and carefully writing down all his behaviors. The list on page 70 is just a start. What behaviors does your dog do that aren't on this list? Be sure not to let your presence affect your dog's behavior. One way to do this is to watch through a window. You could also set up a video camera and leave. Other family members should behave towards the dog as they normally do.

1. Observe your dog carefully for one day. Record his activities using objective terms; that is, write down exactly what your dog does, without trying to say why he is doing it. If your dog greets you excitedly, don't record it as "went wacko," but instead describe exactly what he did, such as "wagged tail rapidly, jumped up on me, ran in two circles, barked five times, placed front legs on ground with rear end still standing." Only record exactly what you can observe.

2. Once you have a list of your dog's behaviors, see how often he does each one. Watch your dog for 10-minute periods at least five different times during the day. Divide each 10-minute period into 30-second intervals. Within each of these 30-second intervals, record each behavior your dog performs during that interval.

3. Now count up how many intervals include a particular behavior. For example, if your dog wagged his tail during 10 of the intervals, place a 10 next to the "tail-wagging" category.

What behaviors does your dog do most often? What circumstances tend to bring about —or stop — certain behaviors? Were the dog's responses different at different times of day? If you have a cat, you can make an ethogram for her, too. How does your dog's ethogram differ from your cat's?

## Body Language

Do you speak dog? You probably do without even knowing it. Like you, your dog uses facial expressions, body movements, and sounds he makes to communicate. He even uses scents. Communicating was very important to the dog's wild ancestors. Body language about who is the dominant animal in a pack of wolves lets its members avoid fighting most of the time. Dogs have inherited these ways of communication. Look at the pictures shown on pages 72 and 73. Do you know what these dogs are saying?

1. "Life is good." Rolls on the ground on his back and sides. Mouth is open and his tongue may loll out. Ears are relaxed. May grunt and groan.

2. "Pay attention to me, please!" Nudges you with his muzzle or places one paw on you. Tail may be wagging slowly. Ears are held forward. Eyes are open wide and he may stare at you.

3. "Want to play?" Rests both front legs on the ground while leaving his rear in the air. May wag his tail slowly and even give a little bark. Mouth is opened slightly, and he stares at you.

4. "I'm #1." Walks stiff-legged and with head and tail held high. May also stand stiffly over anyone he can boss around. Doesn't turn away from eye-to-eye contact. Ears are held forward. May even growl quietly.

5. "I'm a little nervous but I'm not letting on." Yawns in a tense situation. Ears are held back and perhaps down. Tail is tucked slightly.

6. "Please don't be mad at me!" Crouches low to the ground, tucking and wagging his tail. Holds his ears down and licks at your face. Eyes may be squinted, and he avoids eye-to-eye contact.

1. Life is good.

3. Want to play?

6. Please don't be mad at me!

7. I give up! Please have mercy.

8. I'm so scared, I may have to bite you....

9. This is my last warning.

**7.** "I give up! Please have mercy." Rolls over on his side or back and raises one hind leg, exposing his stomach; he may even urinate. Ears are held down. Eyes are squinted, and he avoids eye-to-eye contact.

**8.** "I'm so scared I may have to bite you if you get any closer." Crouches and tries to move away. Ears are held down and back. Head is turned away. May make a high-pitched growl.

**9.** "This is my last warning." Stands erect and moves stiffly toward you. The hair on his withers is bristled. Ears may be forward or back; may growl or bark. Stares right at you.

Dogs have other ways of communicating also. They bark when they are alarmed or want attention. They may howl when they are lonely. They growl when they are threatening. Dogs do a lot of communicating through scent. They have scent glands on various parts of their body, including their anus, feet, tail, ears, and lips. Dogs that meet each other will sniff each other in these places. They will also sniff where another dog has urinated or moved his bowels. Dogs are better at identifying each other by scent than by vision.

**How to SAY IT**

dominant: DAHM-eh-nant

ethogram: EE-tho-gram

ethologist: eh-THOL-oh-jist

How smart is your dog? That's not an easy question to answer. Dogs are super smart in some ways and dumb as dirt in others. Your dog is probably smarter than you when it comes to living off the land, but you are undoubtedly smarter when it comes to solving math problems. Intelligence is made of many different types of abilities, such as memory, problem-solving, and learning ability. Some dogs are geniuses when it comes to doing what they were bred to do, but not so bright when asked to do other things. Then there's the age-old argument: are obedient dogs smarter because they understand and do what you tell them to do? Or are disobedient dogs smarter because they do whatever they please?

## SMARTEST DOGS

According to the opinions of dog trainers and obedience judges, the smartest dogs (in terms of obedience training) are:

1. Border Collie
2. Poodle
3. German Shepherd
4. Golden Retriever
5. Doberman Pinscher
6. Shetland Sheepdog
7. Labrador Retriever
8. Papillon
9. Rottweiler
10. Australian Cattle Dog

## What's a Fair Test?

It's hard to design an intelligence test that's fair for all dogs. Some dogs are just better at learning some things. Retrievers should do well on memory tests, for example, because part of retrieving requires them to remember where one or more birds fell and then go get them. Learning tests can favor breeds developed for tasks requiring them to follow verbal commands, such as herding dogs and retrievers. Problem-solving tests can favor dogs bred to think for themselves when hunting, such as terrier and hound breeds. Such dogs tend to get in more trouble at home. Well-behaved dogs may do poorly because they know that solving problems such as "how do I get the food off the kitchen counter" has gotten them into trouble in the past.

No test has been designed that can really tell you if one dog is smarter than another; all it can tell you is whether one dog is better at that particular test.

## ACTIVITY

# Test Your Dog's Memory

You can measure your dog's memory with some simple tests, given below.

## Short-Term Memory Test

1. Let your dog see and sniff the treat.

2. Let him go with you and watch you hide the treat.

3. Walk your dog out of the room.

4. After 30 seconds return to the room, let your dog loose, and encourage him to find the treat.

5. Time how long it takes him to find the treat.

6. Repeat the test, hiding the treat in a different place each time.

**Note:** Be careful your dog is not using his sense of smell to follow your tracks to the hiding places or sniff out the treats. You can avoid having him follow your tracks by walking all over the area, including to places that look like they might be treat locations but aren't. Does he follow these false trails? You can avoid having him sniff out the area by using a non-smelly treat and placing it in a plastic container, then taking it out when he finds it so he can eat it.

After your dog has practiced the short-term memory test several times, try one of these variations:

## Long-Term Memory Test

Do everything as in the short-term memory test, but don't allow your dog to look for the treat for 5 minutes. If he does well, increase it to 10 minutes, then 15, or even longer. Hide the treat in a different place each time.

## Multiple-Item Test

Instead of hiding one treat, hide five small treats, each in a different location. See how many treat locations your dog can remember.

## Distractions

You know how being distracted can make you forget something. Play a game of fetch with your dog while he's waiting to look for the treat. Does this distraction affect how well he remembers the treat location?

# ACTIVITY

## Test Your Dog's Reasoning

**YOU WILL NEED:**
- watch with a second hand (a stop-watch is best)
- low piece of furniture (just high enough for dog to get paws under)
- dog treat
- large piece of cardboard (or 3 pieces taped together) for Test #2
- scissors

### Reasoning Test #1

**1.** Show your dog a treat.

**2.** Let him watch you place the treat under the furniture. It should be placed so the dog can't reach it with his mouth, but could reach it with his paws.

**3.** Time how long it takes your dog to get the treat using his paws.

**Note:** Some dogs have learned that looking helpless and pitiful makes their people get the treat for them. That seems pretty smart, too!

### Reasoning Test #2

Assemble some cardboard tall enough so your dog cannot jump over it, if possible. It should be shaped or folded like a U, with each arm of the U about as long as (or longer than) your dog's body. Place the U on its side so that the dog stands between the two arms of the U. In the bottom of the U, you need a hole so your dog can peek through. Get an adult to help you cut a hole in the cardboard.

**1.** Have your dog stand inside the U shape. You should be on the other side of the cardboard, at the bottom of the U.

**2.** Let the dog see the treat you have through the hole in the cardboard.

Set up for Test 2.

**3.** Invite him to come and get it. Time how long it takes him to walk around the arm of the U and get the treat. This is hard for many dogs because they have to figure out they must first go away from the treat they are trying to reach.

**4.** Try it several times. Does your dog get faster with practice?

**5.** If you have a baby brother or sister, does he or she do better or worse than your dog at this same test? Note: use a toy, not a dog treat!

ACTIVITY

**YOU WILL NEED:**
- many (at least 20) cardboard or other lightweight panels taller than your dog
- stopwatch
- treats

# Is Your Dog Amazing?

Spatial intelligence means how well your dog learns about his surroundings. A maze is one way to test spatial intelligence, along with memory and learning.

Before setting up your maze, draw it on a piece of paper. It can be a simple maze shaped like a Y in which one arm of the Y leads to a dead end and the other leads to a treat. Make sure the dog can't see it's a dead end or a treat end at the point he decides to go left or right. Even if you want to use a complicated maze later, it's a good idea to first practice with this simple maze so your dog gets the idea.

Before you set up your maze, walk your dog all around over the area the maze will be. This is so your dog's scent is everywhere; it should make it harder for him to solve the maze just by following his own scent trail after he's been through it a few times. You may also rub his scent on the maze walls for this same reason.

1. Set up the maze.

2. Release your dog at the starting point. Place a panel behind him so he can't turn around and escape.

3. If he begins exploring on his own, don't say anything.

4. Give him a good treat and let him out when he reaches the correct place in the maze.

5. If he just stands at the start, go in the maze with him and walk all around it together so he gets used to it. Have a treat waiting for him at the correct spot and let him out. Then try again.

6. Time how long it takes your dog to get to the treat spot. Also record how many wrong turns your dog makes in each run.

7. Repeat until he runs right to the treat.

Make a graph of how long your dog takes to find the treat spot and the number of wrong turns he makes. If you change the design of the maze, does he learn faster the second time? You can compare different dogs, or even compare your dog to a cat or to your baby brother or sister.

TREAT

# D-O-G ESP

Many people think dogs have extra sensory perception (ESP) — perception without using sight, smell, hearing, or any of the other known senses. Some people think their dogs can read their minds. They think if they concentrate on a mental image of what they want their dog to do, the dog will understand and do it. Other people think their dog can sense when they are about to come home, before the dog could possibly hear the car on the road. Here are some activities to test whether your dog has ESP.

## ACTIVITY

**YOU WILL NEED:**
- human helper
- clock
- index cards and pens

## Does Your Dog Have ESP?

### Can Your Dog Read Your Mind?

1. Think of a simple behavior you want your dog to do.

2. In a quiet room with your dog, observe your dog for a minute and record how often he does that behavior.

3. Now visualize (see in your mind) your dog doing that same behavior. Observe your dog for the next minute and record how often he does that behavior.

4. Repeat this five times. Is there a difference in how often he does the behavior when you visualize it compared to when you don't?

### Can Your Dog Predict When You're Coming Home?

1. Have a helper stay with your dog and observe your dog's behavior. Ask your helper to note down any changes in your dog's behavior and exactly when they happen.

2. Leave the place where your dog is and stay away for 25 minutes or so. At the moment you decide to head home, write down the time.

3. Ask your helper to give you his report. Did your dog act differently at the same time you decided to start home? Did he run to the door or window? If so, did he also do the same behaviors at other times when you weren't heading home?

# New Dogs, Old Tricks

Your dog is never too young, nor too old, to learn new tricks. Did you know that much of what we know about learning comes from research with dogs?

## Classical Conditioning

Ivan Pavlov was a scientist who was trying to find out how food affected digestive reflexes. He was studying how dogs drooled when they ate. But a problem arose after awhile: his dogs started to drool before they even started to eat — sometimes they started as soon as they heard the footsteps of the person bringing the food. Those crazy dogs were ruining the experiment! Instead of quitting, Pavlov wondered how hearing footsteps could cause dogs to drool. Here's what he found out: He discovered that dogs learned to associate (link) previously unassociated events using a type of learning now called classical conditioning.

Here's how it works: Before training (or conditioning) some events (or stimuli*) naturally cause a response and some don't. For example, eating food naturally causes a dog to drool, but hearing footsteps does not. If the event that normally causes no response is always presented just before the event that usually causes a response, eventually the dog will respond to both events in the same way. In our example, the dog initially drooled only to food; but after a while he learned that footsteps predicted food was coming, so he started to drool when he heard footsteps.

Both you and your dog learn many different things through this sort of association. Can you think of other examples of learning through association? Your dog

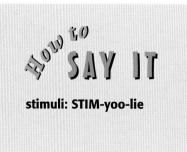

How to
### SAY IT
stimuli: STIM-yoo-lie

Teaching your dog to sit.

probably has already made several such associations, like getting excited when he sees you pick up his leash, or your mom pick up the car keys. Can you teach your dog to respond to something he wouldn't normally care about?

Your dog also learns by discovering relationships between his own actions and their results. This is called instrumental conditioning.

Here's how it works: Your dog naturally performs all sorts of behaviors. He may sit, walk in circles, bark, empty the garbage can, and beg at the table. Some of these behaviors will probably be ignored, some may get him in trouble, but some may be rewarded. Any behavior that is rewarded is more likely to be repeated. For example, if his begging pays off with some tasty morsels, he will be more likely to beg again.

If you give your dog a treat every time he happens to sit, he will sit more often. If you only give him a treat when he sits after you say "Sit," he will learn that sitting only pays off when you say "Sit" first.

**ACTIVITY**

**YOU WILL NEED:**
- many small treats
- wall or corner of a room

# Teach Your Dog to Sit

You can teach your dog to sit without ever touching him. Using a method called shaping, you will reward your dog for getting closer and closer to the sit position, until he's finally sitting.

1. Stand your dog with his rear against a wall or corner (which makes it harder for him to back up).

2. Say "Sit" and show him the treat.

3. Move the treat slightly above and behind his eyes so he must bend his knees to reach it.

4. As soon as he bends his knees, give him the treat.

5. Repeat steps 2 to 4, moving the treat back towards the back of his head so he has to bend his knees a little more each time in order to get the treat.

6. Finally, require him to sit all the way in order to get the treat.

# Working Like a Dog

Dogs and people have worked side by side throughout the centuries. Dogs have helped people find and catch food, control and guard livestock, get rid of pests, guard the family, pull cargo, help fishermen, and save drowning people. In the Middle Ages, people used lapdogs to attract fleas off the people and onto the dogs! Along the way, people found that just having dogs around made them feel better. Simply petting a dog reduces blood pressure in people. In general, people who own a dog or cat live longer than those who don't.

**Earning Their Keep:** Although most dogs today are valued most as companions, many dogs still earn their keep by performing valuable jobs. Some breeds have been performing the same jobs since they were developed.

- Border Collies can control hundreds of sheep, directed only by the shepherd's whistles and their own good sense.

- Livestock-guarding dogs, such as the Anatolian Shepherd, keep predators away from sheep on farms.

- Hunting dogs point, flush, or retrieve birds, or track foxes, raccoons, rabbits, and other small mammals.

**New Jobs:** Dogs are versatile and adaptable. They can be found parachuting from airplanes, checking out suitcases on conveyor belts in airports, riding ski-lifts to get to avalanche victims, and directing their visually handicapped people through a maze of city subways and streets. Dogs love their new jobs just as much as they love their traditional jobs.

- Search-and-rescue dogs may search miles of wilderness for a lost child or sniff through tons of rubble for a buried victim. Well-trained dogs can locate a person from a quarter of a mile away, or find someone buried under snow, rubble, or even under water.

- Many dogs are trained to sniff and search out planes and buildings for bombs, search suitcases for illegal drugs or food, and even sniff around homes for termites. No machine has ever been found that can compete with the dog's sense of smell.

- Therapy dogs are like therapists in fur coats. They visit hospitals, nursing homes, mental health facilities, and prisons, where they can give people unconditional love, motivation to communicate, entertainment, and someone warm and cuddly to hug.

- Service dogs help people who are physically disabled. They may pull a wheelchair, pick up dropped objects, open doors, or make a telephone call in case of emergency.

- Dogs have been used to guide blind people for centuries. Today, guide dogs are specially trained for this purpose. They help people travel safely and live independently.

- Dogs can also give confidence to deaf or hearing-impaired people. These dogs alert their owner when that person's name is called or when they hear the alarm clock, telephone, doorbell, or fire alarm.

- One of the oldest jobs of dogs has been that of warrior, fighting side by side with their masters. War dogs serve as sentries, patrols, scouts, mine detectors, tunnel detectors, and messengers. These dogs have saved countless lives.

- The police dog, or K-9, is one of the most valuable officers on the police force. Who else can run down a fleeing suspect, locate crime scene evidence, sniff out contraband, and control a crowd? Many K-9s have given their own lives in the effort.

## KING BARKER

If dogs can do it, there's probably a contest to see which one can do it best. One of the strangest and noisiest contests of all is the barking contest for the Finnish Spitz. Barking is so important to the way this breed hunts in its native land that a king barker is crowned every year in Finland!

## IDITAROD

It's been called the last great race on earth, but the first race was the greatest one of all. The year was 1925, and Nome, Alaska, was in the throes of a deadly diphtheria epidemic. They were out of vaccine and snowed in. Against all odds, dog teams raced 674 miles for life-saving vaccine. Lead-dogs Togo and Balto became celebrities for their heroic efforts. Their mission is celebrated in the annual sled dog race that retraces their trail — the Iditarod.

# PART 4

# Your Dog's Health and Functioning

You and your dog can do many things together. Taking care of her health is an important part of caring for her. She'll be a happier and healthier friend because of you! You can be prepared for an emergency, know how to keep her cool, learn some danger signs, and maybe even save her life. You can teach her to jump a barrier and learn how she uses those four feet of hers to walk, run, and gallop.

Your veterinarian should give your dog a complete checkup at least once a year. You can help your dog stay healthy in between by giving her home checkups and noticing how she is behaving. The checkup can be combined with a fun activity for both of you — a massage.

# How to Give a Doggy Massage

One of the best parts of having a dog is petting and stroking him. You can make it good for your dog's health by turning your petting into a massage. Massaging your dog can ease his sore muscles, help him relax, strengthen the bond between the two of you, and may even help with certain behavioral problems.

Before you start: Use your own body to try out different massage techniques. Use different parts of your hands, such as the palms, fingertips and knuckles, along with different pressures ranging from very light to gently hard. Move your hand in different patterns, such as in large or small circles, straight lines, or move one finger at a time. Move at different speeds, from relaxing slow-motion to invigorating high-speed.

Have an adult help you the first time you massage your dog. If your dog is upset by any of the massage techniques, try another one or quit altogether. Watch your dog for cues that he likes what you're doing. Find a quiet place and have your dog lie down, with you sitting beside him. Each of the following steps should take about 15 to 30 seconds.

1. Start by simply placing your hand on his body. Remain quiet and relaxed.

2. Start talking or singing to him softly. Think of a tune and use your dog's name in it.

3. Now glide your hand down his back from his neck to his tail. Continue stroking, taking turns using both your hands. You can come back to this step throughout the massage session, varying the pressure or speed of your strokes.

4. Use your fingers and palms to rub his thighs in a circular motion. You can sometimes use a little harder pressure in this area.

5. Next move to the shoulders and upper arms. Use your fingertips and knuckles to make small circular or waving motions.

6. Move to the forechest and use your fingers or palms to make circling, waving and gliding motions — whatever your dog seems to like best!

7. Cup your hands around the top of the neck and make gentle squeezing motions as though you were kneading dough or clay. Move up and down his neck.

8. Gently use your fingertips to make small circles and pressing actions on the top of your dog's head.

9. Use your fingertips to make small circles on your dog's cheeks.

10. Gently rub up and down your dog's throat from his chin to his chest.

11. When you're ready to stop, rest your hand on your dog and talk or sing to him, just as you did when you started.

# Check Your Dog's Health

While you're massaging, keep an eye out for signs of possible problems, such as:

- abnormal lumps on or under the skin
- matted, dirty, or smelly hair
- redness, sores, or bald spots
- parasites or black "flea dirt" (little spots that look like pepper but are really flea excretion plus blood)
- dirty, reddened, or smelly ears
- red, swollen, or runny eyes
- runny nose
- swollen, misaligned, or cut toes
- broken or overly long toenails
- dirty, loose or broken teeth
- bad breath
- weight gain or loss
- noisy breathing or coughing

Ask an adult to look at anything unusual you find.

# First Aid

If your dog is hurt or suddenly becomes ill, you may need to help her. Practice now what you will do.

1. Stay calm. If you get upset, it will upset your dog and only make things worse. Speak to your dog calmly.

2. Do not endanger your own safety trying to help. Don't run in front of cars, get in the middle of a dogfight, or jump in deep water. You could be badly hurt. If you are hurt or in danger it will only make it harder for your dog to be saved.

3. Get an adult's help as quickly as possible. Do not get in a car with a strange adult, however. If possible, call your parents. You should have your veterinarian's emergency phone number programmed in your phone or written down next to it; call him for help.

4. Try to get your dog to a safe place only if it's totally safe to do so. If she is hurt, she may try to bite without thinking. You can tie a sock or rope around her muzzle so she can't bite, but only do this if she is breathing normally.

5. Keep your dog as quiet as possible until help arrives.

6. While waiting for help, you can perform the ABCs of first aid:

   a. Airway. Is she choking? Could she have something like a ball or piece of food stuck in her throat?

   b. Breathing. Check to see if she is breathing. Is her chest going up and down?

   c. Circulation. Is her heart beating? If you press on her gums, do they turn pink again?

Be prepared to report your findings to the adults when they arrive. It is possible to perform CPR on dogs, but you need special training. Your family may wish to attend classes for both human and canine CPR so you will all be prepared in an emergency.

# Hot Dogs and Cool Canines

You and your dog may not agree about what temperatures are most comfortable. Large dogs, as well as dogs with thick fur, tend to get hot very easily. They enjoy cold weather and some even like to sleep in the snow. Small dogs, especially shorthaired ones, are just the opposite; they get cold very easily and prefer to lie in the sun.

## Fur Facts

Thicker fur insulates the dog against the cold and keeps her body heat in. In hot weather, her body heat builds up inside and can't escape into the air because the fur traps it. Thin hair allows body heat to escape and provides very little protection against the cold.

But why do big dogs tolerate cold temperatures better than small dogs? It has to do with the ratio of body mass to body surface. More body mass builds up more body heat; more body surface area lets more body heat escape. The smaller a dog is, the more body surface he has compared to his body mass.

## Muzzle Meaning

There's one other very important trait that helps a dog lose heat: the length of her muzzle. Dogs don't sweat through their skin like people do; the only place they sweat is on the pads of their feet. Sweating helps keep people cool, because the water that evaporates off the skin surface helps the body lose heat. Your dog also cools herself by letting water evaporate, but she lets it evaporate off her long tongue and the inside of her nose. The longer her tongue and the longer her muzzle, the greater the area she can use for cooling. Dogs with pushed-in faces get overheated very easily.

A dog that is really hot will have a swollen, red tongue, because more blood is sent to the tongue so the blood can be cooled and then help cool the rest of the body. A really swollen tongue is a sign that dog is overheated.

## How Hot Is Too Hot?

Because running builds up heat, you shouldn't make your dog run when it's hot outside. Dogs that run in hot weather can have a body temperature as high as 108°F (42.2°C)! If your dog has been resting, her temperature should be about 101° to 102°F (38.3 to 38.9°C). That's higher than a person's normal temperature, which is around 98° to 99°F (36.7 to 37.2°C). If you think your dog is too warm, ask an adult to take her temperature. This can be done with a rectal thermometer. If your dog's temperature is under 100°F (37.8°C) or over 103°F (39.4°C), alert an adult. If it's under 99°F (37.2°C) or over 104°F (40°C), you will probably need to call the vet.

Dogs can die if they are overheated. That's why it's very important to make sure your dog has a way to stay cool in warm weather. Never leave a dog in a closed automobile, where the heat can rise very quickly.

### KEEPING WARM IN COLD PLACES

Dogs that were bred to live in cold climates tend to have thick, double coats for insulation and fairly large, rounded bodies. They also have medium-length muzzles and short, thick ears to minimize heat loss and the chance of frostbite. Sled dogs often burrow in the snow to sleep. The snow traps their body heat in their fur, so it can't escape to the outside, and they stay warmer.

## Cooling Down

An overheated dog needs to cool down quickly. The best way to cool an overheated dog is by putting wet cloths on her and letting a fan blow over her. You should take her to the vet right away and then keep her quiet for the next day. Be extra careful that old or sick dogs don't get overheated or chilled.

# Run, Spot! Run!

You and your dog move from place to place in quite different ways. You use only two legs, while your dog uses four. Your dog can move his legs in more combinations than you can. His main ways of moving, or gaits, are the walk, amble, pace, trot, canter, and gallop. Unlike humans, dogs walk and run on their toes only (no heels) most of the time, which helps them go faster. However, at a full gallop, the "heels" of the front legs of very fast dogs do touch the ground. The ancestors of dogs and wolves needed to run down their prey, so speed was crucial.

## From Walk to Gallop

**Sequence of dog walking.** The walk is the slowest speed. When the dog walks, she usually has one leg off the ground at a time. The other three legs are usually on the ground.

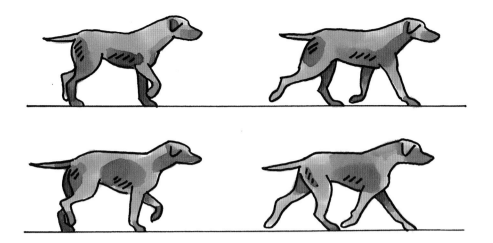

**Sequence of dog trotting.** The trot is the next slowest common gait. When the dog trots, the diagonal legs move together; that is, her right front and left rear move as a pair and her left front and right rear move as a pair.

**Sequence of dog cantering.** The next faster gait is the canter. It's hard to describe how it looks, but easy to describe how it sounds: it is called a three-beat stride because you hear three footfalls, then a silent pause, then three footfalls, then a silent pause, and so on. That's because two diagonal legs move together as a pair while the other two diagonal legs move independently.

**Sequence of dog galloping.** The gallop is the fastest gait. If you listen to a galloping dog, you can hear four footfalls. In most galloping dogs the feet move in the following order: left rear, right rear, left front, right front (or its mirror sequence: right rear, left rear, right front, left front). All four feet are off the ground at the same time when they are all contracted under the dog's body.

**Sequence of Saluki using the double-suspension gallop.** Some really fast dogs, like Greyhounds and Salukis, also fly through the air with all four feet off the ground during the time the feet are fully extended in front of and behind the dog. This type of gallop is called a double-suspension gallop, because the dog is suspended in the air twice during each stride.

# Watch Your Step!

A dog's stride is the distance between the point where one leg hits the ground and the point that the same leg hits the ground again. You can measure her stride at different speeds and different gaits to see how it changes. You can also measure it in dogs of different shapes and sizes. How does leg length affect stride length? How about body length? Is there an ideal height and length proportion for the longest stride? How does her stride compare to yours?

1. First you need to train your dog to run beside you at the speed you want. You may have to throw a ball or treat to get her to gallop over the sand or sidewalk — otherwise you may not be able to keep up with her!

   a. If you are using sand, have her walk and run over the sand and measure the distance between her footprints. Smooth out the sand between runs.

   b. If you are using cement, wet her paws before she runs and then quickly measure the wet pawprints she leaves before they dry.

2. The hard part is identifying which paw you are supposed to be measuring!

   a. In sand, try several practice runs until you're good at identifying the correct footprint. In most dogs, the rear feet are smaller and narrower than the front feet, so you can identify them that way.

   b. On cement, you can just wet the one foot you're measuring, but then you'll miss half the fun of seeing where all the feet go.

3. Do you notice that as your dog runs faster, her feet tend to move toward the center? When she's running full speed they will be in almost a straight line!

4. Do a run yourself. Watch how your own footprints tend to move in toward a centerline as you go from a walk to a run. Try running without letting your feet move toward the center. You wobble from side to side and won't be able to run very fast. The same is true with dogs, and it's one reason fast dogs have narrow bodies. They don't wobble as much when they run.

5. You may wish to make a videotape of your dog moving at different speeds. Be sure to tape it from a low level, so you can see her legs. Play the tape in slow motion to see how her feet are moving.

# Jumping For Joy

Have you ever run an obstacle course? Police dogs and army dogs train on tough obstacle courses, and dogs competing in the sport of dog agility also run obstacle courses. Most dogs really love it and have a lot of fun as long as you don't ask them to do something they can't do.

You can make your own doggy obstacle course in your backyard. Ask your veterinarian how high your dog should jump; puppies, fat dogs, lame dogs, pregnant dogs, and old dogs should not jump at all. Warning: never teach your dog to jump a height that is higher than your fence and never practice by having your dog jump any fence. You don't want to teach your dog how to escape from the yard!

**High jumps:** If you have a picnic table with benches, turn two benches on their sides for two hurdles that are about a foot (30 cm) high. Start with the hurdle very low, and raise it after your dog is clearing the present one easily.

**Tire jumps:** If you have a tire or even a hula-hoop, you can teach your dog to jump through it. Start by having her step through a tire whose bottom is resting on the ground. Raise it gradually. Tie the tire on four sides so it doesn't swing back and forth and injure your dog. If you use a hula-hoop, you can hold it by hand.

**Broad jumps:** You can use a cushion from outdoor furniture to teach the broad jump. Some dogs will just step right on it, so put crinkly newspaper on top. Most dogs don't like to step on newspaper when they are running or jumping. You can also use several big sticks laid next to each other. Gradually move the sticks farther apart so there are gaps between them. The dog should learn not to step in the gaps, but to jump over all the sticks. Put newspaper between them if he tries to step there.

**Tunnels:** Children's play tunnels are great for dog obstacle course tunnels. You can also make your own tunnel using big cardboard boxes opened on two ends, or by draping sheets over several pairs of chairs lined up in a row. Make the tunnel as short as possible at first, so your dog can see how easy it is to go through. You may need a helper to call her through with a treat at first. Gradually make the tunnel longer — you could even put a turn in it.

**Slalom course:** A slalom course is one where the dog weaves in and out of a series of poles, the way skiers do on snow. The easiest way to make your own is to use 3 to 6 toilet plungers standing upright and placed in a row. Start with them pretty far away from each other and use treats to guide your dog through them. Gradually move them closer to one another and try to go faster.

If you can't make an obstacle course, don't worry. Your dog doesn't care so much what you do with him as long as you two do it together. So put down this book and go play with your dog!

# Careers with Dogs

Maybe you would like to have a career with dogs one day. You could be a veterinarian, veterinary technician, dog behaviorist, dog trainer, dog groomer, dog breeder, show-dog handler, scientist researching dogs, artist specializing in dogs, or author writing about dogs. You could design and sell toys, clothes, and equipment for dogs; have a pet supply store; work for a dog food company; or run a doggy day-care or boarding kennel. You could train dogs to assist blind, hearing-impaired, or handicapped people or to provide therapy to the elderly or handicapped. You could train dogs for police or military service or to detect illegal items or even termite-infested homes. You could be a hero by joining search-and-rescue groups and finding lost people and buried victims. You could compete in dog shows, field trials, obedience, agility, and tracking competitions. You could help save a breed from extinction. You could devote yourself to humane causes, help combat dog overpopulation, and fight cruelty to animals. You could become a lawyer specializing in animal law and legislation. Or you could be a pioneer and come up with a totally new dog career. Here are some topics you can look under at the library or on the Internet to learn more about dogs:

| | | |
|---|---|---|
| Dog health | Dog care | Canine search and rescue |
| Dog behavior | Dog training | |
| Dog breeding | Dog breeds | Dog physical therapy |
| Dog grooming | Dog toys | |
| Veterinary | Dog supplies | Careers with dogs |
| Dog competitions | Dog shelters | Service dogs |

# About the Author

D. Caroline Coile holds a Ph.D. in psychology, with research interests in the behavior, neurophysiology, and genetics of dogs. A former researcher and lecturer at Florida State University and Kenyon College, Caroline specializes in clarifying technical concepts. She has written 19 books and more than 200 articles about dogs. Her books include *Barron's Encyclopedia of Dog Breeds*, *Show Me!* (a book all about showing your dog), as well as breed books about Greyhounds, Jack Russell Terriers, Chihuahuas, Golden Retrievers, German Shepherds, Pit Bulls, Australian Shepherds, and several other breeds. Her book *Beyond Fetch* is about fun games to play with your dog.

Her writing awards include the Bryan Robinson Neurological Award, the Dog Writer's Association of America's Maxwell Award and Denlinger Award, and the Eukanuba Canine Health Award.

Caroline travels extensively to dog events and has lectured throughout the country. She has appeared on several radio and television programs, including National Public Radio's "Talk of the Nation," ABC National Australia's "Breakfast Radio," and American Health Network's "Ask the Veterinarian." She lives in Georgia with a houseful of dogs, all Salukis.

Photo by Patty Sosa.

The author with Wolfman, a prize-winning Saluki.

# Index